The Longest Furrow Volume 3

By Frederick Charles Waterfall

First Published May 2011
© Fred Waterfall Publications (Countryman) 12.10.2013
mail@fcwaterfall.co.uk

> Dedicated to the memory of our son
> **Matthew**

All money raised from the sale of these books goes to
**Headways North Staffs.
The head injuries' charity**

Index

Chapter
1   Cattle Droving
2   Our First Attempt at Silage making
3   Embarrassing Moments (Bike)
4   Dairy Cows of Old
5   The Load Tipped Over
6   The Five Village Green Cottages
7   The Garden Telegraph Pole
8   Other peoples rubbish can be so interesting
9   There's a mouse in the house (or more)
10   Another Hedge Cutter Mishap
11   I've got a little Breakdown
12   The Wedding Reception
13   The Suckler Cows have started Calving
14   Memories of Olden Days
15   The Village Policeman
16   Self Sufficiency
17   I had an encounter with an A10 Tank Buster
18   People and Families Born in this House.
19   It happened one fine summer afternoon
20   The Dentist
21   Irreversible Changes in one Small Village
22   Up to now we haven t had a Drop (rain)
23   Mother made her Pastry (1940's)
24   Fields lanes, n Country Roads have Names
25   Black Gold
26   The Longest Swath
27   The War time Blackout
28   I'm Not an Educated Chap
29   Loading Cattle
30   Computers Read the Lot
31   We have a Cow and she's Real Mad

32	The hay elevator
33	Cattle out Wintering
34	The Persistent Escapee (cow)
35	Story of Hobble End Cottages
36	Low Cost Production, Milk Marketing Board
37	The June Returns 1961
38	Rats
39	First Land Rover a "Rag Top" Diesel
40	Farm Dispersal Sales
41	Mother reared her Chickens, in the 1940's
42	Potatoes planted foot apart not twelve inches
43	The two hundred day winter
44	Garry the bull (1996-2008)

Chapter 1

Cattle Droving

At one time cattle were always driven to market; sometimes miles away in the local town, and nearly every house or cottage had a garden gate that could be shut as the cattle were herded by.
Then from the market they were herded again to the slaughter house (although there was often a slaughter house adjoining the sale yards) or out to whoever had purchased them if they were stores.

Father recalled the time when he was driving a few bullocks into market, and whilst walking down a side street in town, one bullock saw an open shop door, and it decided to hop up the step and went into a shop. Being only a very small shop there was nowhere to turn round as the counter formed a passage where the customers stood.
The old lady behind the counter screamed with astonishment as the beast filled her shop, the bullock struggled to turn round to make an escape, in doing so it pushed the counter and all things behind it across and up to the goods on display along the back wall.
This trapped the shop keeper; the bullock did what came natural and lifted its tail and plastered the counter and wall with muck then hopped out to continue its walk to market.

In our village there were seven herds of cows that all travelled and walked out to distant pastures each day and back for evening milking. The small holding with about twelve cows crossed the path of four herds, first he would if not careful he would travel along a hundred yards of road that the Yews farm cows walked, then pass across the path of the Green Farm yard where there cows emerged, then past Church Farm where both herds walk to the same lane, then at the ford those two herds crossed the path of Village Farm herd. Three herds walked down the same cow lane branching off into their respective fields.

The two herds at the other end of the village crossed paths and were walking the same two hundred yard stretch of road, but in opposite directions, so a regular time for turning the cows out was most important.

    For some reason the Church Farm cows were very late on being brought in for evening milking, and met with the smallholding cows coming out in the opposite direction down a narrow stretch of road near the ford. Forty two cows heading south and twelve cows heading north.

The forty cows (heading towards the church, Church Farm.) got strung out into a single line or as near as cows do, so the herd of twelve cows were walked steadily through being tapped gently to remind then which direction they supposed to go and after about five minutes both herd continued on their way not having "lost" any to the other herd.

At the ford there is a narrow brick foot path bridge for pedestrians to cross, and the majority of cows preferred to go over the bridge as the bottom of the ford is very stony and hard on their feet.

In the next village a farmer there always went to Ireland to purchase fifty or more store bullocks each spring, these came over on the ferry to Holly Head where they were loaded onto railway wagons.

Cattle wagon on the railway were couple next to the steam locomotive, the wagons being loose coupled they sprung and slapped the buffer as the brakes were applied and when power was put on to start pulling. This ricocheted down the length of the train, the smoothest ride was next to the engine.

His cattle were unloaded at the station yard in the village until it was closed by Dr, Beaching, (The government minister in charge of reforming the railways at that time, he cut off many branch lines and closed many local stations) then they had to unload further down the line at the station in town

From there they were walked about six miles back to his farm, by this time they were tired and hungry from the journey, so could be seen snatching grass as they passed through our village stopping for five minutes at the ford to water them.

So cattle droving did happen in England, but in a quite minuscule way compared to cattle drives over the pond

While milking early one morning I had a phone call from the railway signal box at the next village to say some of our cattle were on the main railway lines. This is a busy line with four tracks two north bound and two south bound. It was a group of ten big incalf heifers, they had ventured through the railway fence where it had burnt the wooden post from an embankment fire and were standing grazing on the opposite embankment.

In the 1960's trains were nearly all pulled by diesels a few goods trains were still steam. Two trains had already stopped from north and two from south, everyone stuck their heads out of the carriage windows to see what had halted their journey. The cattle were recovered from the opposite embankment between the four locomotives, and ushered back into their own field.

Cattle on the Railway Line.

One morning while milking cows,
A phone call came from railway man,
It was the Bridgeford signal box,
Reported cattle onto line had ran,
He put his signals onto caution,
Don't worry drivers on "visual", will run
We race off down the Moor Lane,
To cattle grazing in the morning sun.
Two trains they had already halted,
And two more rolling to a stop,
They left a gap through which to drive,
Cattle back to embankment top,

The Four *lengthsmen helped and a driver,
And hundreds of people watched,
Three express trains and one commuter,
Why their journey scotched.
Cattle hopped cross four main lines,
And back into the field,
Embankment fire had burned a post;
Rail fell down a gap revealed,
We thanked the drivers and local men,

For their quick advance,
Fast line trains do speed at seventy,
Cattle wouldn't stand a chance.

Lengthsmen; railway workers, looked after length of track, usually 3-4 miles per group of six

I must say that this is a very busy stretch of line, and is the main London to Scotland main line, the Royal Scot(1950's) steamed past at full speed very day at about three o'clock and back to return to London in the early hours of the morning. Many of the steam express trains were pulled by named engines.

(Of the parallels between the railways and the church) Both had there heyday in the mid-nineteenth century, both own a great deal of Gothic-style architecture which is expensive to maintain, both are regularly assailed by critics, and both are firmly convinced that they are the best means of getting man to his ultimate destination
Reverend W. Awdry (1911-1997)

Chapter 2

Our First Attempt at Silage Making

The grass came out near black and toasted, but smelt sweet with the molasses, the cows liked it, but not much feed value left in it.

    The first silage that we saw demonstrated was at our local Farming College in the 1950's, they had a concrete tower silo that was loaded with a tractor driven cutter blower. This was hand fed by a man with a pitch fork, and was blown up to the top of the tower and let to settle with its own weight. It was of coarse dangerous to enter a silo after it had stood for a few hours as the gasses would build up.

    A notice on the side of the tower pointed this out and only after the blower had been run for a while was it safe to enter. It had an external ladder shrouded in to get access to the hatches that are sealed as it was filled or opened as it was unloaded.

Unloading was a heavy job as it had all got to be dug out by hand, one good thing was that the grass had been chopped short much like the double chop forager produce today.

    It was then pitched out of the nearest hatch, to fall down the covered in ladder acting like a chute, it also needed a reliable man at the bottom to load the silage onto a cart or barrow, and if it built up in the ladder chute the un-loader was trapped. It made excellent silage as the height provided the weight to compress the forage, but was very labour intensive.

At home our first attempts at silage making were very crude to say the least, the silo was a welded mesh wire formed into a circle with sisal paper (tarred paper) pegged to the insides, when the first six foot had been filled another six foot ring was mounted on top and continued filling. Mown grass was picked up from the field from windrows with a green crop loader, stacked on a trailer and unloaded by pitch fork into the wire mesh silo.

When the two tier were filled and well trampled down, it was capped off with ground limestone. Needless to say it over heated; it was long 'as cut grass', with added molasses, and was impossible get solid enough and exclude all the air. The grass came out near black and toasted, but smelt sweet with the molasses, the cows liked it, but not much feed value left in it.

This shows the back end of the green crop loader,

The next spring we had an earth scoop for the back of the tractor (Fordson E27N) and dug a silage pit up in the middle of the grass fields that were shut up for mowing. The grass was picked up with the buck rake from the windrows, in fact we had two, and taken directly onto the clamp, it was a lot more successful as we could compress it with the tractors as we went on.

A couple of men were on the clamp with forks leveling the grass and adding the molasses. Again it was capped off with lime which when it got wet formed a good seal. The silage was dug out by hand, cutting six foot squares with a hay knife, and loaded by hand onto a trailer.

This is a hay knife, used to cut blocks of loose hay from a bay or a stack, it was more difficult to use in silage.

We had a couple of years doing it as described above, then we had a David Brown Hurricane Harvester and two tipping trailers fitted with high sides
The trailers had screw jacks and a block of wood to go under the foot and hitched and unhitched with a drawbar peg to the forage harvester and then to the towing tractor, the hydraulic was a screw connecter in those days.

A larger silage pit was dug back at home the trailers ferried up and down the road, by this time the additive was in the form of a powder to help neutralize the fermentation of the grass. The consolidation of the clamp was with the buck rake tractor and with the grass being short, flailed, and direct cut; it was heavy and green consolidated easily. Plastic sheeting was just coming in to cover the top and a layer of soil was spread to weigh it down, other things were tried for holding the sheet down, then eventually settle with car tyres then eventually plastic sheeting was put up the sides completed a better seal. At this stage it was still being unloaded from the pit by hand.

It was not until we had cow cubicles that the silage clamp moved inside a purpose made shed that it became self-feed, where by a barrier with a long spiked foot at the feed face was buffeted into the face each day for the cows to brows adlib. By this time, 10 years on, we had progressed to a Class Jaguar off set double chop forager and six ton trailers.

When I started farming on my own for a while I had a self-fill continental type silage trailer which cut the crop as it went through the pickup reel, but it was pitifully slow at unloading and with only one trailer running up and down the lanes with each load it only lasted two years before I got rid and went back to flail harvesting.

And on up to date our silage is made into round bale silage and stacked in a convenient place ready for winter feeding

Field Names of Seighford

Out in Britons countryside,
Looks like a patchwork quilt,
Of roads and lanes and field tracks,
Evolved and some were built,
They lead from towns and villages,
And farms, map nailed on beam,
Each field a hedge and ditch and gate,
Watered by pond or stream.

The fields both large and small have names,
You wouldn't dream exist,
Some relate to owner past,
And others the type of land persists,
Red Rheine's is one of these mean fields,
When ploughed reveals red clay,
Unless the frost into it gets,
No seed bed though you work all day.

Best known one I've no doubt,
Behind Yews farm is Cumbers,
Ten houses built along the village,
Take that name and numbers,
Down by the ford is Mill Bank,
Four acre few trees by the brook,
The Hazel Graze another great name,
Nut bushes to make a crook.

Fosters by the railway line,
Named after a soul long gone,
And Pingles also down the Moor Lane,
That defiantly is a mystery one,

Noons Birch is the most beautiful name,
One that congers' you mind,
Public Field it was part of the land ,
Run to the pub up back and behind.

Hoble End is another nice name,
Where two cottages stood in the fields,
No track did they only footpath,
Lonely place only a well and concealed,
Moss Common a field where the ditch,
Springs in the middle to pick up,
It is important that they are there,
To water the ewes and the tup.

Ash Pits are three fields in a row,
The Big the Middle and Little,
Ash trees are the obvious reason,
And only one pit in the lot,
Hanging Bank is most sinister name,
It's a cold north facing bank,
More research into this is what's needed,
But all we've drawn is a blank

Lanes to the fields also have names,
Moor Lane runs way from the ford,
Connecting with that is Love Lane,
A grassy rut track half way Bridgeford,
The Oldfords Lane goes up to the farm,
To Coton not a short cut by car,
And Smithy Lane runs way through houses,
The shortest of all by far.

Moss Lane is one that runs eastwards,
Cow lane that it is can be seen,
Grass up the middle and is long,
See cattle grazing fields so keen,

It has path that runs up it,
And gates shut on each end,
The path is quite long;
It comes out near Doxey on bend.

**Knowing trees, I understand the meaning of patience.
Knowing grass, I can appreciate persistence.**
Unknown

Chapter 3

Embarrassing Moments bike

Over the years you build up a clutch of embarrassing moments or events.

An early one I recall was with my relatively new bike (bicycle), when we were younger we always yearned for a new bike, but had to make do with an old one cobbled together from the good bits of other bikes, some of which were recovered from a pit hole at the side of the airfield, where the RAF dumped their unwanted or unusable bikes. I must say here that the pit was full of water, and we had to go with a rope and a homemade grappling hook.

Some of the bikes we recovered had better wheels and sometimes a good chain and seat than what we were using, so our highbred bikes were so called cobbled together. It was not till after I left school and started earning a wage that I persuaded my parents that I ought to splash out on a new bike. This they sanctioned and was now proud owner of a Raleigh bike with three speed hub gears. It was kept clean and not used on cattle droving, (where we over took galloping stock on our old bikes down the main road in order to turn them into the correct fields). It was not used to go scrambling through woods and fields and ditches, it was only used for serious cycling.

I had had this bike for two years or more, when I was asked to move a tractor and its silage trailer from our home farm to Church Farm at the other end of the village, so the "new" bike was deposited into the back of the trailer and carefully laid on its side so as not to damage or scratch it. Of course it got forgotten and within a few minutes the trailer was filled with a full load of three tons of grass, and then tipped over an eight foot drop into the empty clamp. (Without me knowing, this had the effect of shortening the bike by about two feet) I was working the buck rake and ran backward at speed into the load to open it up then proceeded to stack the grass until this one buck rake full had part of a twisted wheel protruding from the grass, on further investigation it dawned on me what had happened. It was my New Bike, my pride and joy, one of the first purchases I had ever made. On recovering it, there was not a straight bar left all, it had been crumpled, the best demolition job I had ever done; and not done a better job of destruction in all the sixty years since. I hid it and dare not tell anyone. I was overcome with embarrassment, as the men, (four of them) and my brothers, working on the farm would rib me mercilessly.

It was quite a few years before I admitted as to what had happened to it, and it remained hidden most of that time, I cringed every time I thought about it.

This is how I would describe the sort of bikes our gang of village lads rode.

I had a Good Old Bike

Remember years ago,
when I had a good old bike,
Its mud guards loose and rattled,
new one I would like,
The brakes were none existent,
rims they had a dent,
And wobbled as I rode it,
the wheels they were bent.

The seat was ripped and torn,
springs showing through,
A Saddle bag was hanging,
off two little straps askew,
It had a carrier on the back,
with long and snappy spring,
A clip to hold my jacket down,
save tying on with string.

———————

The Puncture Outfit

I had a puncture outfit,
in a tin four inches long,
It had a pack of patches;
they didn't look very strong,
A tube of tyre solution,
there to glue the patches down,
Sand paper to roughen,
and talc in glue it turned brown.

I often had a puncture,
when I went over spike or thorn,
Turned it upside down to find,
the tyre is well worn,
Off to fetch two table spoons,
out of the kitchen draw,
Just to use as tyre leavers,
see that mother never saw.

The tyre off the spoons they bent,
muck and dirt abound,
Pulling out the inner tube,
the hole it must be found,

Clean it up and roughen,
peel the patch and stick right on,
Blow it up, only to find,
we've only got another one.

Tyre mended blown up hard,
now to have some fun,
Standing on the peddles hard,
make the old hens run,
Up a hedge bank down a track,
riding through the wood,
Good job it's just an old one,
sliding through the mud.

———————

What breaks in a moment may take years to mend
Swedish proverb

Chapter 4

Dairy Cows of Old

Milked by hand some cows had teats almost as thick as your wrist, with front teats sticking out "east west".
Dairy cows of old, bore little resemblance to the dairy cows of today. Back in the 40's every herd had its own bull often reared out of one of your own cows, served by a neighbours bull, which was boasted to be the best in the neighborhood. Blood lines and pedigrees' meant nothing when you had a fine looking bull running with the cows, however what came out of the "pot" was very often a different picture.

This you would not find out until you had used the bull for three years when the first heifers calved down and came into the milking herd. Up until that period in time; most herds were milked by hand and cows with teats almost as thick as your wrist were common place, and front teats sticking out "east west". Pendulous udders in the older cows, with udders only inches from the ground, these were kept on because perhaps they were easy milkers and perhaps the highest yielders. Some of these cows were almost impossible to milk with a machine; the thick teats were not too bad as long as all four teats pointed "south". Some cows had low back quarters and empty looking front quarters, which did not suit the machine milking, I remember a big "duck stone" would be place on the claw of the milking machine, and then a cord would be over the cows back to hold the units up onto the front teats. Often the udder would be so low it was almost impossible to reach down to even get the units on.

Father started his herd by exchanging a sow for a cow

around 1930 progressing on to a few more cows in small buildings with a cow shed and fifteen acres next to his father's farm. Then he married mother and they took on a farm near the edge of town where he was able to expand his herd. These would be a bit of a mixture of breeds including shorthorn and a few black and whites and everything in between. Most of the milk went in Churns on the train into Birmingham and some mother made butter and cheese which was sold locally to shops or at the door. Then at some point the dairy started sending a lorry to pick up the churns from each farm, probably when the Milk Marketing Board was first set up.

We Had an Old Butter Churn

We had an old butter churn,
it was on a wooden stand,
A big handle on the side of it,
to turn it all by hand.
The lid it had sight glass,
valve to vent the air outright.
Lid clamped on with three screws,
clamps it up real tight

Mother turned the handle,
till butter grains appear,
Drain the butter milk,
rinse n' wash grains to till clear,
Add some salt and knead them,
butter pats for this,
Packed into grease proof paper,
on hot toast its bliss.

It was mid 30's that father broke his arm and that meant he could not milk cows by hand, and it was around this time that the local machinery dealer had got the first milking machines in. They were keen to get a machine installed on farms in their patch, and father decided to go for one, he bought an Alfa Laval four unit outfit.
Of course it took a bit of getting used to the new way of milking, and did not help that a lot of the cows had "rough" udders not particularly suited to the new teat cups.

Father got impressed by the herd of cows that the neighbour ran, these were pure bred pedigree Ayrshire's, most of his cows had nice small uniform well placed teats and compact udders that stretched forward under the cow's belly. On looking at them from hand milking point of view, it would be finger and thumb milking, but this was the era of the milking machine, these cows looked as if they were designed for it.

When we moved farms up into the village the herd could be expanded, and along with his old neighbour they went up to Carlisle to the pedigree Ayrshire sale and between then bought a lorry load of incalf heifers, this would total I think about twelve, the cattle wagons were not as big as they are today. This they did for the following few years, one of the last loads that came down were polled, they had no horns, these were the first we had ever seen and they were bullied by the cows with horns. You may have seen old pictures of Ayrshire cattle, their horns curled up pitch fork style, and they knew how to use them. To remedy this father spoke to his vet and he had all the cows horn cut off. As the cows were all tied by the neck in stalls it made it easy to restrain them, first the vet tied string tight round the base of the horn to act as a tourniquet and I cannot recall

whether they were injected with pain killer.
The instrument for cutting was a huge pair of shears with five foot handles, and the grip of three men to close them. A barnacle was put on the cow's nose and a cord held by another man while the operation took place.

Barnacle is local name for this gadget for holding a cow by the nose, the rough drawing below gives you an idea of how its opened, by drawing a spring up the shank to open the jaws, then place it in the nose and let the spring go, it been such a long time since I used ours that I cannot find it to photograph it.

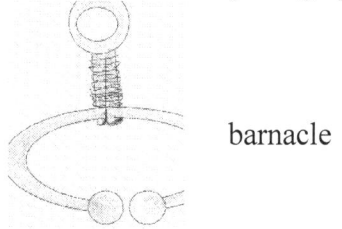

barnacle

The ring at the top is for a rope, then you can hold an animal the same as you would hold a bull by its ring, I can tell you they don't appreciate it at all, and it has the benefit of taking their minds what you are actually going to do at them. They made rapid progress down the shed doing about twenty five cows, and on some cows the string had rubbed off letting the blood flow readily, squirting high into the rafters of the cowshed, it took a couple of hours for the vet to stem the flow from first one cow and then another.

When the calves were born, each calf's horns were cleaned with a fluid to remove any hint of grease and a type of glue applied called "colodian" this ceiled the horn bud and in effect dehorned the calf. It was a bit hit and miss some calves having one horn of in some cases both horns, it all depended on how clean the bud was when the colodian was applied, and how old the calves were, they had to be done in the first few days after birth. This went on for two or three years when a pair of dehorning irons were bought and the horn buds were burnt out ensuring that no horns were missed. These were heated on a blow lamp one being heated while one was in use, and the forerunner of the modern gas dehorning iron.

It was predominantly Ayrshire cows that made up the herd for the next twenty years, when the British Friesian cows with modern udders and higher yields and father started using a Friesian bull through artificial insemination on the Ayrshire cows. In the 1950's the Milk Marketing Board start the improvement of cow confirmation, by the use of Artificial Insemination, and monitoring the progeny born this way to provide proven bulls. Over the following twenty years or more the udder and teat confirmation improved and where everyone had more than a cow or two with curled up toes and deformed feet, these were improved as well. Then in the following twenty years again saw the tremendous improvement in yields, and this coincided with new improved management techniques such as cubicles self-feed silage and parlor milking, and a changeover to Friesian cows.

Father ran a Dairy Herd

Father ran a dairy herd,
of mainly Ayrshire cows,
These were housed traditionally,
tied in stalls in rows,
Brought down for milking,
had to be tied with a chain,
Each knew their own stall,
a left and a right contain.

Cows were used to standing,
to their own side of the stall,
They would part to let you in
between when you call,
A bowl full of corn, and in
with the bucket and stool,
Milked by hand while they're eating,
good job when it's cool.

He was one of the first to try,
Newfangled milking machine,
A vacuum pipe was installed,
New motor and pump had to be,
Four buckets and a spare,
Four cows milked nice and clean,
This was quicker by far,
Once the cows got used to routine.

Milk was cooled in the dairy,
With water from the well,
The dairy collected it every day,
Had to be cool to sell,
The fridge was a copper heat exchanger
Hanging on the wall,
On top a Dee shaped receiving pan,
Fresh milk we poured it all.

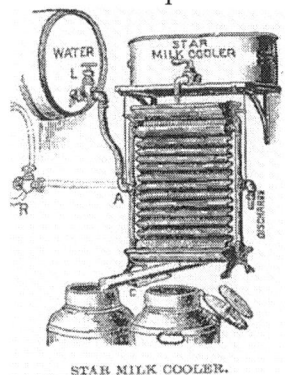

STAR MILK COOLER.

Well water runs on inside the fridge,
Milk run down outside,
Churns were filled for the dairy,
To a measured mark inside,
Labeled with where it's to go,
At one time went by train,
Now a lorry picks up the churns,
From a churn stand on the lane.

Thirty years milked this way,
In churns milk was poured,
Restricted now by the number of stalls,
Yields he did record,
Bulk tank came and a pipeline too,
Milk tanker every day,
This took Father to retirement,
Very modern to do it this way.

Ayrshire cows always had a noticeably better butterfat level that could be seen in the milk bottles that it was sold in, Friesian cow on the other hand were often down to 3% fat, with the "blue water" up from the bottom 97% of the bottle. Because father had just the odd Friesian cow in his herd, when asked "why keep a Friesian cow in a herd of Ayrshire he always replied "We wash the shed down with her milk if the well runs dry"

Cheese - milk's leap towards immortality.
Clifton Fadiman (1904 - 1999)

Chapter 5

The Load Tipped Over

It was as if the tractor was on an elastic band springing gently from its precarious position, with me holding its balance,
You may or may not know that feeling when you know a trailer that you just spent a lot of time and energy loading by hand tips over. Set the scene, it was 1960, I was fresh from Farm College and had set out farming on my own fifteen months before. A seven acre field of seeds hay had been down in a week of good weather and we had just baled it. The tractor was my International B250 with a three ton tipping trailer suitably adapted to carry bales, the side boards had been taken off, and an extension fitted to the rear end to extend the floor area and what we call gormers fitted front and back(uprights at each end of the trailer) to support the load.

Half the field had been shifted and this load had been loaded from the lower end of the field, the balance of the trailer was dramatically altered by having an extension out the back so less of the load was on the drawbar. To enable the tractor to pull the load up the slope to the gate I set off diagonally across the field and progresses steady without wheel slip. The load was firmly roped on and being carried on only one axle (it being a tipping trailer) it swayed with every small indent of the field, in this one area of the field was a burrow (fox or badger) with a mound of soil spread out from the excavation, so I decided to go top side of it burrow but how wrong I was. The tractor was well past the burrow when the wheels started to slip, the trailer still along the side of the slope. I thought I was well clear of any possible collapse, then the wheel sank as the lower side wheel of the trailer was carrying ninety percent of the load, it was a slow motion where you could see it happening and could not stop it. The whole load tipping sideways in one whole block, well roped together it took the trailer with it, the only thing it was still hitched to the B250 on the ring hitch hook. Just as the load finally touched down still enblock it lifted the top side rear wheel of the tractor two foot off the ground just by the twist of the ring hook, this again was slow motion, by this time I had put it out of gear and had move to a position on the side of the tractor as that of a sailor in high wind, trying to counter balance the impending disaster.

It was as if the tractor was on an elastic band springing gently from its precarious position, with me holding its balance, one of those times when things happen quickly, but in very slow motion in your mind, it seemed to be hanging for ages, hanging off the side of the tractor then I reached for the hydraulic lever and lowered the hook, which gently lower the tractor back onto the ground releasing the trailer.

There was ninety six bales on the load and every one had to be left on the ground while the trailer was righted, no damage was done other than the ring on the trailer drawbar had now got a permanent slight twist by which it had lifted the tractor. There is nothing more annoying than having to do a job twice, and with me driving I was the one to pitch the bales back onto the load. By pitch I mean pitch with a pitch fork, and seeds hay baled firmly they were heavy, and towards the end of the day when the whole field could have been cleared, but for the mishap.

I drove this tractor from new in 1956, It stood unused for almost twenty years, and now it is fifty years old, it's been brought back to life. This is it after a few months' work on the engine, new mud wings fitted and the wheels painted. See how weathered and green the back end was, it looked in a sorry state when we first pulled it out to do it up. That's still the same ring hitch hook under the tractor by which the over turned trailer lifted its rear wheel well off the ground.

My Old Tractor -International B250

My old tractor standing there,
For years it's not been started,
Drove it myself from new,
And now almost departed,
Roof is now blown off the shed,
And it's rained in down its pipe,
The engines well stuck and rusted,
On the inside full of gripe.

Over fifty years that I have had it,
While working never faltered,
Apart from rust and lack of paint,
Appearance never altered,
Got to save it now before,
It rots and rusts away,
To pull it out and look at it,
Do it straightaway.

Some tyres flat and perished now,
But they will hold some wind,
Enough to carry it to shed,
Where it can be re-tinned,
Off with bonnet wings and wheels
Can see it undressed now,
Get into heart of engine see,
If can put it back to plough.

Water in two cylinder,
Have rusted pistons solid,
Sump comes off to loosen;
Big ends then are parted,
Hammering and thumping,
To get the pistons out,
New set of liners n pistons now,
Cheque book it's time to clout.

Got new shells for big ends,
And set of gaskets too,
Back together now and see,
What there is next to do,
Injector pump with lid off,
Is pushing up stuck springs,
With little bit of persuasion,
Knock down plunger fittings.

New injectors they are fitted,
Valves are well ground in,
On with lively battery,
To turn it mid smoke and din,
Firing up it comes to life,
From near scrap recovered,
Can concentrate efforts now,
Look better newly coloured,

Bought new wings and new nose cone,
Old ones full of dents,
Standing on its jack stands,
It's far from those events,
Gunk and solvents' liberally,
To wash the oil and dirt,
Lying on your back beneath,
And get all on your shirt.

Ready for the primer now,
And get in all the corners,
Always find some bits not cleaned,
Drips along the boarders,
Rub it down where paint has run,
Ready for its top coat,
Don't want dust or flies or any damp,
Gloss I must promote.

Front and back wheels now back on,
Brand new shiny nuts,
New exhaust enamel black,
Tin pan seat to rest your butt,
Fit the loom and lights and switches,
Oil gauge and ammeter,
Needs new steering wheel and nut,
To set it off the neater.

Out on road run we have booked,
Got a logbook too,
On red diesel it runs at home,
Some run on white a few,
Insurance and a tax disc now,
New number plates as well,
Will miss my cozy heated cab,
Frozen Christmas tail to tell.

———————

This is the old tractor now, just about like new, we have not got hold of a new steering wheel yet, or the headlight's, it has taken part in a number of road runs and light work about the farm. As always in pictures, it's what's in the background that interests most folk, such as the Fordson E27N set of steel wheels, and on the right a Fordson Elite plough.

Seeing as its hay we were carting---

Hay is more acceptable to an ass than gold.
Latin Proverb.

Chapter 6

The Five Village Green Cottages

Church Cottage.

This is one of a pair of cottages known as "Spight" cottages, supposed to have been built to prevent a view, from the old vicarage to Seighford Hall. The occupants of the Hall did not get on with the vicar. The earliest people I remember living here were Mr. and Mrs. Breese, who were the parents of Mini Clark, Flossy Brown, Vera Doughty, and one son, Percy who was a motor car mechanic at Bridgeford Garage for Herbert Bennion. They all lived in the village, and when old Mrs. Breese died in the 1950`s, Sam and Lotty Fox moved in, moving his pigeon loft and tool shed from the old thatched house on the west side of the church

Sam Fox and his Wife Lotty

Old Sam Fox and his wife Lotty,
Lived in the old Church Cottage,
Sam he was a tractor driver,
To earn his weekly pottage,
This he did at Green Farm,
On a Fordson TVO,
Steady progress all day long,
When out to reap and mow.

A tall thin man five foot ten,
His clothes hung loose around him,
Hung his head forward and looked at you,
Underneath his hat brim,

Could not turn his head,
Looked round with his sharp eyes,
Perfect stance for using,
His twelve bore with his demise.

He wore a long grey smock,
For eve-ry occasion,
On his bike into town,
In the belfry did not loosen,
His boots with spats,
Rarely got into the muck,
So careful was old Sam, not quick
enough to make quick buck.

He had brown piercing eyes,
Through bushy eyebrows looked,
Quick spoken man was he,
Fast response as he joked,
What little smile he had,
Turned his thin lips almost level,
Two little creases either side,
Midst his talking babble.

Lotty his wife worked hard,
In her Churchyard cottage,
Took in washing half the week,
From houses in the village,
Her washing line always full,
All the way down her garden,
Dried and ironed and folded up,
And parceled in her kitchen.

The smallest lady in the village,
Smoked woodbines all the day,
Washing money kept her in fags,
The shop she went to pay,

In the pub sometimes she called,
Had a drink bought for her,
Nothing strong to make her wobble,
Just a half of beer.

House cleaning too was on her menu,
Bucket brush and mop,
If she came across a bottle ,
Only took a drop,
When she stood to have a natter,
Leaned heavy on the brush,
Lit up her fag to have a drag,
On woodbines she had a crush.

She always wore about the village,
Cross-over pinafore,
Tied around the middle,
Hem almost to the floor,
Her skinny legs and wrinkled stockings,
Plus the ankle socks,
To reach when ironing with her fag,
Should have had a box.

Their garden it was tended,
With the greatest care,
Produce for the larder shelves,
A few flowers and roses flare,
Grassy path down the middle,
Wash line tied from house to tree,
Hedge all trimmed and tidy,
Brick path swept to outside laver try.

Sam had not retired so long
When he passed away,
And Lotty kept on working ,
In her quaint old way,

Bought her fags one at a time,
As she got some money,
Called at the pub most dinner times,
With her nose so runny.

Everyone respects her courage,
Working to the end,
To keep her woodbines in her fingers
She would sometimes lend,
Always paid back a little later,
Next week do the same,
Moved to Smithy Lane bungalow,
And end her working fame.

Along the churchyard hedge of Church Cottage were two very large lime trees, these were blown down in high winds, one just skimming the side of the house, dislodging only a few tiles. This happened relatively recently, in the early 90's, and took some time to clear up and settle the garden down again.

Ivy Cottage

The second of the "Spight" cottages, was built at the end of the vicarage drive, sister cottage to Church Cottage. This was a farm cottage to Yews Farm, and lived in by the cowman Mr. Hill, until he retired and moved down the road. Albert Hine moved in with his family, and was wagoner for the Yews Farm. There he grew tobacco, among the many things he grew in the garden, until he retired when he moved into one of the new council houses in Bramall Close.

This is Ivy Cottage on the end of the vicarage drive with Church Cottage (the other "Spight Cottage") on the right in the picture with two big lime trees can be seen towering over its roof, it looks as though they had been "crowned " (topped off) back in the 1950's, forty years later they blew down in a high wind narrowly missing the cottage.

I Remember Albert Hine
Dated in the 1940's and 1950's

Albert was a Waggoner,
For Charlie Finnimore,
A strong and healthy man he was,
And stood at five foot four,
In his younger days it's told,
He would walk out of the hills,
With a ewe under each arm,
In winters cold and chills.

He lived at Ivy Cottage,
Where he grew his own bacca (tobacco)
For to keep his pipe alight,
It was not a laughing matter.
As the summer days got longer,
So pick leaves did he,
And hung then in the living room,
The ceiling could not see,

When dry and almost crisp they got,
Into a draw he pressed
To keep them through the winter,
By large old chimney brest.
He rang church bells on Sundays,
With a team they were so loyal,
they practice in the mid-week night,
As if expecting royal,

He had a box, of twelve inches,
Though he was in his prime,
The little man he rang the tenor,
Keeping stead time.
The team with him at that time,
They are well remembered,
It written in the belfry sill,
Names and bells all numbered.

All day he worked with horses,
A carting muck with two,
He had the one up in traces,
As the load was from the Yews,
Up to the Noons Birch field,
Where he hooked it out in rucks,
Ten paces up, ten paces wide,
So even was the muck.

Describe the man were looking at,
A jerkin he did ware,
Tied round the middle with binder twine,
To hold more than just a tare,
Corduroy trousers tucked in spats,
Round his hob nail boots,
Cap raked left and pipe raked right,
Pouch and matches in a box.

His old waist coat worn and tatty,
Kept his big watch n matches dry,
The shirt it had few buttons ,
And the collar he kept it by,
For high days and holidays,
When everything was clean,
And home guard duty,
When the sergeant, he was very mean.

His platoon was made up of men,
Who worked around the farms,
they mustered in the village hall,
To train as fighting men at arms,
The pork and bacon beef and taters,
Butter eggs and creme,
All of these were traded,
Mongst the brave old fighting men.

Albert kept his pipe and bacca,
It was woodbines for the rest,
As the smoke it was so dense,
No room for enemy they jest
This ploy worked well, no men got lost,
And warmer they could keep,
Til sergeant came and caught them,
So loaded up his jeep.

Two cows he kept and young stock,
And a few old tatty hens,
The fields where he kept them,
Had sheds and tidy pens,
He mowed along the grass verge,
All the way to Stafford,
To make his hay to keep them,
And drew water from the ford.

All his life he worked dammed hard,
But slower he did get,
Albert met his maker,
He was one you can't forget,
Popular and cheerful,
He lived to seven,tee
Buried in Seighford church yard ,
Remembered by me and thee.

The two cottages across the road (the left front door in the picture) was lived in by Alf Worthington and his sister. Alf always worked in town in an office, his sister also had a clerical job.

The house next door was occupied by Violet Ashley a widow, and used to deliver the newspapers. She would be up at six o'clock in a morning, and walk down to Great Bridgeford to the post office, to collect all the papers needed for Seighford. These she carried in an old push chair this job took her till about nine o'clock. She was attacked and molested on a couple of occasions and from then on always carried the pepper pot with her, for protection. Violet wore thick lens glasses, like the bottom of bottles, and read the paper three inches from her nose. On her paper round she always had her old gabardine mac on, along with her black beret with a chimney on top. She was a tall, slim old lady who walked quite briskly and very straight in posture. The biggest drawback with Violet was, that when she talked to you, it was you who needed the mac, as she talked with quite a splutter.

She was seldom ill and rarely missed her round, but one Saturday she fell down the stairs and broke her leg. No one missed her on Sunday as there was no papers to deliver, and it was not until she dragged herself down the garden path to the wicket, that she was discovered, after some fifteen hours on the floor. She was taken Stafford General Infirmary, where she had a difficult recovery, but never delivered another paper.

I Remember Violet Ashley

Violet lived in a cottage,
Next but one to the school,
Lost husband Bill some years ago,
Life had been so cruel,
For years now she delivered,
The magazines and papers,
Carried them on an old pushchair,
Even in bad weather.

She walked over the bank,
All the way Great Bridgeford,
Collect them from the paper shop,
For very little reward,
This she did six days a week,
Every week of the year,
Bout four miles it was the round,
She talked and got some cheer.

When she spoke you needed cover,
For she talked so quick,
With not many teeth, she
shplashed and lisped all as if in panic,
This is when she met everyone,
And carried all local news,
Gossip she spread in record time,
To anyone she choose.

Violet wore an old gabardine mac,
With black beret on her head,
Carried old umbrella too,
On her feet bootee's worn out in the tread,

Her hair was cut with beret on,
Clipped short up to its brim,
Beret had a chimanee on top,
Wet weather not looked quite so trim.

Some time ago Violet got attacked,
When collecting paper money,
This did not deter old Vi at all,
Reported to the local bobby,
Now she carries a good defense,
Her pepper pot in pocket,
Carried it for years in case,
And never did find a culprit.

When she'd finished her round one Satdee,
Fell and broke a bone,
Wasn't found till late on Sunday,
She crawled out to her gate alone,
This was then end for poor old Violet,
Never walked again,
In the village everyone missed her,
Not long was she in all that pain.

Blacksmiths Cottage.

This was a tied cottage to the blacksmith. Here lived Mr. and Mrs. Bill Appleby. Bill was a blacksmith in town; his forge was in County Road, opposite the old Stafford General Infirmary, he did no farrier work (horse shoeing) but did mostly fabricating and fancy iron work.

Mrs. Appleby was the school caretaker; this was very handy, as she had only to walk the length of her garden path. This is Mrs. Appleby's daughter standing where the school playing field gates are now, taken around late 1950's. Their garden was all where the car park is on the front, by the school. The footpath from Coton Clanford came over the Cumbers fields from the Oldfords and right through his garden, bringing the kids from all points south of the school. This cottage had a few outbuildings for the odd cow and a pig sty, and an outside privy, opening out onto about two acres of paddock which is now the school playing field?

This is the school as it is today, at one time it had iron railings along the front to protect the narrow garden where you see the green shrubs. The Blacksmiths cottage was between the end of the school and the pair of cottages (now all one house) you see on the left of the picture. The right hand end of the school was the School House. A huge new block of class rooms have recently been built to the rear, over what was the school garden.

A sense of curiosity is nature's original school of education.
Dr. Smiley Blanto

Chapter 7

The Garden Telegraph Pole

The long arm of the hedge cutter whiplashes forward past the pole and back again, giving the flails a second bite at it.

It was July and the front garden hedge was looking a mess, and with it being in the Centre of the village, and on the village green and next to the school and church, we like to keep it tidy by trimming it three times in the season. Being almost a hundred yards in length, the hedge was in easy reach for the tractor hedge cutter, so this is how it's done. So on with the hedge cutter for the first time this year, taking great care on reversing up to it, (you see the tractor has got a very sharp clutch), it takes a good half hour to fit to the tractor, with all the controls and PTO and stabilizing wishbone, run it up to test it, then out onto the road to make a start.

The first run along the shoulder of the hedge, included lifting out a little round a telephone pole, so I go gently inch up to it.

(That's the new pole with the cable running up this side) Then another few inches, but the tractor lurched forward six inches, (the sharp clutch you see) stab the brakes and the head of the cutter out on its long arm whiplashes forward over a foot past the pole and back again, giving the flails two bites at the pole. (A new set of sharp flails had not long been fitted. Up my side of the pole was an underground cable rising to the top of the pole for distributing telephone wires to the school headmaster's house and the lecturer at British Telecom, also the vicarage and the school, the vet, but not our house.

Our garden hedge runs up to the school, that's it on the right and that's the new pole with the cable running up this side of it. Two inches had been plained off this side of the old pole along with rising the cable. The head of the machine was perfectly vertical, but not quite out of the hedge enough to clear the pole cleanly. So the few inches forward turned into a foot and it chewed into the pole like a planning machine in one swift movement, and twenty yard up the road was a four foot length of twenty four strand cable, in shreds. Although it was in a very public place, no one saw what happened, so in consultation with my assistant, we drew a large grain trailer close on the pavement by the pole to hide what we were looking at, and proceeded to examine the possibilities. One, we tried was to pull the ends to meet and twist the colour coded wires together, so we pulled the cable down the pole a little way, then proceeded to pull surplus cable out of the conduit from under ground One huge heave and it would not budge, but all the insulation stripped off the cables. This option not being possible we hid the broken wires behind the pole, and gave up, thinking that we could blame the council grass verge trimmer who had passed through a few days prior.

All this happened on a Friday evening, no one complained about the phones being off until Monday morning. The Telecom, man at his house was away sailing, the Vet was on duty, and had a quiet weekend, the vicar was busy, and the school was closed. A new eighteen point computer had just been commissioned at the school and a direct on-line internet connection via Telecom set up, and I had cut it off.

I spent all Monday morning carting muck, past the scene, to see what developed. A junior technician arrive at 10.30am and could not find the fault , a more senior technician arrive and did no better, the area manager arrived and found the fault and guessed what happened. I made myself scarce and went a long way around to arrive in our yard for lunch so as not to go past the pole. By this time the area manager had worked his way down the village talking to Reg at the blacksmith's shop, and when I drove by on the tractor Reg innocently pointed shouting that's him, that's him.

I had been rumbled, and even the council verge cutter story did not wash, two weeks later I received a bill. The junior was £28 an hour, the senior man was £42 an hour and the area manager was £84 an hour, and £12 worth of new cable, it came to almost £400 (which was claimed off my insurance). Then two weeks later they came and replaced the old pole and put in a new one, this time they run the cable down the back of the pole. I asked for the old pole but they declined, if I had had to pay for the new pole I would have insisted they leave me the damaged one, but I thought I'd better not push my luck, they obviously did not want to reward "flagrant" damage.

I Remember the New Telephone Pole

Decided garden hedge need cutting,
Out with flail cutter,
No small thing on big tractor,
One wheel was in the gutter,
A pole it stud right in the middle,
Blocking my clean run,
The tractor has a clutch so sharp,
Think formula one the race begun.

I pull right close up to the pole,
Six inches, to myself I said,
Lift the clutch, the rev were sharp,
A foot it whipped the head,
Up near side of pole was wire,
To the school out of a hole,
It ripped clean off four foot of this,
And dug right in the pole.

The wire we did run retrieve,
From way off up the road,
It contained twenty four wires,
Easy matched up all colour code,
So with strength we tried to pull,
More wire out of hole down there,
With sudden pull we stripped the lot,
And had to leave them bare.

For two days over weekend,
The neighbours had no phone,
While carting muck out through the yard,
Out away from home,

Telephone van drove slowly by,
He didn't find the fault at first,
So he called out senior,
who couldn't find it, all was in a mist.

Area manager he came by,
Spotted pole with chunk out split,
Wires he found and came to look,
For who he thought was culprit,
Taking notes he did asked the question,
Did you do it with stern report,
Yes was my reply,
I will bill you for repairs wire pole and labour.

The minion who did come the first,
Had set upon repairs,
A lorry with new pole arrived,
Up lifting pole in the air,
Asked for old pole to be left,
For me to use at home,
That is not our policy,
To encourage damage to our poles,

The bill did come, minion's price,
Twenty eight pounds hour,
Senior's price but nil he did,
Forty two pounds for all his power,
Area man was double again,
For he did find the fault,
It added up to quite a sum,
New pole made it tidy by default.

Policy now is give wide birth,
And fit new clutch the tractor needs,
School computer newly fitted,
Wall more close with shorter of leads

Vet across the road on duty,
Had a quiet weekend tend his dog,
And I did work and sweat and fret,
To tell the man it was bad fog.

Experience is a marvelous thing that enables you to recognize a mistake when you make it again.
Franklin P. Jones

Chapter 8

How other peoples rubbish can be so interesting

It's funny how other peoples rubbish can be so interesting, everyone looks at what would not fit into your dust bin.

Now take a skip that you will pay through the nose for and given the chance most people will want something you've thrown out, or on the other hand may in the dead of night add to it. When you have the room to store things for future use, or it is too good to throw away, or been out dated by so called a better product, you keep it in case the new one breaks down.

In the back of our outhouse is an Electrolux vacuum cleaner, these are the bomb shaped ones that you drag along on two skids with the pipe. I remember when mother had this new, she could fill the bag in one session almost without moving the plug to the next socket (in the back kitchen where we took our boots off).It was when we kids were too young to dry our own hair, out would come the Electrolux, and the vacuum pipe would be attached to the other end and after a few minutes of running it would blow nice warm air. It was by chance that if you bumped the cleaner or its pipe when on its hair drying cycle, and you were the first one, you may have to wash your hair again. For 40 years of its 60 years life it has hung on a six inch nail (which is rusting away and needs a new one) in our shed on standby, in fact it was brought out recently to help clean the soot out of the Rayburn, and before that we had a Jackdaw stuck in the chimney and used it to get the worst of the mess & soot up. It still blows hot air out tuther end but unless you want to get rid of your grey hair, I would not use it.

Another item uncovered was an old washing

machine, one with the wishy-washy paddle and a mangle, the mangle would in fact swing over your sink, to squash out for rinsing from what you have washed, or stay over the machine to recycle the soap suds for the next load. Monday mornings over breakfast time, you could hear the Burco boiler struggling to get the first ten gallon of water singing and eventually boiling, amid clouds of steam this would be ladled or bucketed into the ADA wash machine, in would go all the whites along with the soap flakes. By 9.30am the whites would be on the line on a fine day, and the next load of washing put in.

Meanwhile the leftovers from yesterday's Sunday lunch (it was always double veg, taters mashed with cabbage, carrots and coli, as father prepared it on a Sunday morning) were sizzling in a huge frying pan, popularly call bubble and squeak with cold beef with pickles'. On Mother's washing day, she had not much time to prepare a meal and this was regular Monday fayre . When it began to smoke it was time to turn it over in the pan, and heated in minutes.

Mother's Monday bubble and squeak

At lunch time every Monday,
Mother made bubble and squeak,
Potatoes' and cabbage and other veg,
Sometimes even a leek,
All ingredients left over's from Sunday,
Put in big pan to fry,
Crisping on the bottom then turned,
Plenty of heat apply.
Cold beef sliced and put on plates,
Contents of pan dealt out,
Pan was a big one, it had to be,
Six plates to fill no doubt,

Pickled onions and pickled red cabbage,
Went with this a treat,
All homemade stored in big jars,
Made the meal complete,
Jug of gravy thick and hot ,
Often a skin on top,
All of it devoured with relish,
Plates cleaned off the lot.

Mother would be getting all the overalls out of the washing machine, a good three hours after she had started work. The water that was drained out into a bucket from the machine was dirty, so dirty and silty that another bucket or two were used to rinse it out clean. With bits of straw and chaff a bit of stick was kept at hand to clear the drain tap if it blocked. It's still runs, and was brought out at times when our modern one burnt out or broke down, it was never brought in to use as stand by, but used on the back yard by the outside hot tap. It's never been out for seven or more years so it's ready to be chucked now.

Every item you trip over in the back shed has a history, in the first stride there is a very old electric motor, this used to drive an old potato riddle that had been converted from hand wind to motor driven. It also has a push button switch box bound with tape and string, the health and safety people would love that. The wooden riddle has been gone now twenty years ago infested with woodworm, although we do have its cast iron fly wheel knocking about somewhere.

A cast iron pig trough, big enough for a sow and litter

is making the foundation of a small scrap pile alongside the wall, not having been moved or used since we stopped pig keeping some twenty eight year hence. It is a bit chipped but still useable.

A cylinder head off an old tractor that had been replaced and stored, this tractor eventually set on fire way down the fields, when it got over heated. I remember climbing onto the top of a load of hay that it was pulling off the meadows, when I saw smoke. A spark from the exhaust had set it on fire, and I got up just in time to grab the handful of hay that was smoldering and put it out. I uncoupled the tractor, and it took more time for me to call the fire brigade (I was half a mile down the fields) than it took them to come from Stafford. No mobile phones then.

Hanging on the wall is an old scythe, I doubt if many people could even sharpen one properly now. This one has a binding on the shaft where at some time it has been weakened or cracked. Or more likely run over with a cart wheel. It has a long blade, and was used to cut the first swath from round the corn fields to enable the binder to do the first circuit without running down the growing crop. Shorter blades were used to badger (cut the grass) the hedge banks when the hedges were cut by hand. The hedge and grass cuttings were collected and used to keep the frost off the mangol hog during the winter.

On one of the lofts are a set of sale sticks, six still wrapped in brown paper brand new for a Massy Harris binder, and a couple of sales as well. Also a set of binder canvases, these had been well used, it was always important to keep these dry particularly during storage.

It looks as if the moths have had near on fifty year of chewing at them and are now only patterns if someone wants to make replacements. Father always rode the binder, firstly with three shires pulling it, then his standard Fordson, which as school kids we were conscripted to steer and drive when corn cutting. Every now and then we could not recover from a steep turn at the corner, and put a wheel (or more) into the crop, this would prompt a savage scowl and if a whip was at hand as in the horse days, this would have been used liberally on us.

Looking up in the beams of the shed are two old combine blades, sixteen foot long. These are dangerous thing if left where they could trip you up. They had been worn away so much sharpening, that a new blade was ordered. The carriers would only carry a parcel maximum of twelve foot so that was the length that came. Four foot of the back bone of the old blade was cut off and welded on to the new one to make sixteen foot, and new sections riveted on. The old combine went on for a few more years before being scrapped. (See "My old combine" story).

On the wall in the old dairy is the rack on which you used to hang all the milking equipment to steam the lids and rubber pipes. Other items such as milking buckets lids, pulsators, sieves, churns, a vacuum pump, a vacuum gauge, none of which have been used since milk went into bulk tanks over forty years ago. The rubber pipes and liners have badly perished now, but all the metal items are still as used, and usable. The area in the shed next to the dairy has the outline in the floor where the old coal or coke fire boiler stood, and you can see where the pipes went through the wall to the sterilizing chest. In here the larger items such as buckets and cooling fridge and receiving pan would be sterilized, no chemical cleaners in the early days.

In the loft was a long three inch drive barn shafting going from wall to wall with bearings at each end set in the wall, and one in the middle carried on a fancy cast iron bracket. These had bronze bushes and an oil cap for lubrication. Along the shaft at the drive end was two pullies, a fast and loose one, as in the days of the first hot bulb open crank engines could not be started under load. The belt drive would be diverted onto the loose pulley to start the engine and a stave of wood used to bring in the drive by pushing the live belt onto the fastened pulley and bring everything into work that was belted on the other five pullies. There would be a chaff cutter, a root pulper, a cake crusher, a roller mill, and of course the milking vacuum pump. All of these original machines have gone except the last one, not all would be used at the same time. When electricity came into the village a large electric motor was fitted in place of the open crank engine. Again this would drive all the machines in the barn one or two at a time.

In one of the back sheds is a cow shed lost in a time warp, it still has its brick coble floor and oak cow stalls, blue brick mangers and wooden racking across the front of the stalls, and a fodder bing along the front. Where the cow chains fasten to the stalls, they slide up and down an oak stave, and in the nineteen forties a vacuum line was added, along with self-fill water bowls it also has a low loft, As it happens no items for storage (rubbish) have ever been stacked in that shed, so apart from swallows and the odd farm cat having kittens in there, it still remains the same.

In the loft above this small cowshed was, I was told, at one time the village mortuary, where if anyone from outside the village who died or was killed would be taken to await burial. It had a set of brick steps leading up to the loft door from the pub (the Holly Bush) side of the building. In my memories of this room/loft it was always used as a store for the pub, for crates of bottles and the like.

Around the yard are four heavy cast iron wheels, this is all that remains from a wooden elevator of the 1920's era. My predecessor (the bloke who farmed here before me) used to thatch a roof onto it every year when they had finished harvest. But when bales came in, it got set on one side and forgotten. I took to it as a heap of rotting wood and thatch, and some iron fittings and wheels. Each wheel weighs about 85kg (in my speak that's about a hundred weight and half). Two front wheels are slightly smaller than the rear.

Some more iron wheels about the yard were off a Massey Harris corn drill, these are 4'-6" tall and was a drill that could sow fertilizer as well as the seed corn. It was the absolute bees knees around 1950, later, twenty years later, they were fitted with rubber tyre wheels. Unless they were well looked after, the fertilizer rotted and corroded the metal hopper and spouts. The wheels out lasted the drills, and now set around the garden as ornaments.

The older I grow the more I distrust the familiar doctrine that age brings wisdom.
H. L. Mencken (1880 - 1956)

Chapter 9

There's a mouse in the house (or more)

We often get winter visitors;
They come in from the cold,
They find a little hole or two,
And squeeze through being bold,
Then look for food and hide away,
They come into our house,
Who can blame them I'd do the same,
That crafty little mouse.

Can hear them chewing under the floor,
Middle of the night,
The very board bed stands on,
A hole right through not quite,
And running along the water pipes,
So warm to their little feet,
Nesting in the airing cupboard,
In kitchen find crumbs to eat.

You're lucky if you see one,
ya can see where they have been,
Chewing at the cornflake box,
For food they're real keen,
Whole family of them hiding,
Wait for us to go to bed,
then rummage round, find some food,
Attack the loaf of bread.

The cat he knows where they are,
But he's old and doesn't care,
Our dog she sniffs and finds them,
Hiding under the stairs,
Barks and make a real loud noise,
But come out they will not,
So all the livestock live together,
I think **we've** lost the plot.

———

The best laid schemes o' Mice an' men, Gang aft agley,
An' lea'e us nought but grief an' pain. for promis'd joy!

(**The best laid plans for mice and men, oft go awry, And leave us nothing but grief and pain, for promised joy!**)

 Robert Burns (1759-1796), To a mouse
(Poem,   November,1785)

Chapter10

Another Hedge Cutter Mishap

I had a bit of a rush to get all the hedge cutting done before the end of February, and then in the last five minutes of finishing for the year, on drawing in the cutter head in towards the tractor, got distracted and it flailed off the whole of the back light cluster and ripped the plastic/rubber mud wing to shreds and left a cable with seven wire sticking out all ready stripped of insulation but about two foot too short to reach a new back light (DAM BLAST & BUGEGRRRR) that was a bit mild to what I was thinking.

I have had one or two close shaves with the back light before over the years, taking off the lens, or just chipping it, but this cleared the whole site , good job it did not get down to the back tyre.

This is what the rear end of the tractor used to look like

Living Hedgerow

A variety of plants,
in the hedgerow,
Se what is growing,
and living below,
Food in the fruit,
for birds and the bees,
Shelter from the weather,
beneath the trees.

The rabbits dig burrow,
and birds do nest,
Hedgehogs roll up,
in the leaves to rest,
Toads and spiders,
wasps and hornet,
All of them living,
along in this thicket.

Hawthorn and hazel,
maple and elder,
All help to make up,
the variety of splendor,
Briers and Rose hips,
with berries bright colour
Crab apple and sloe,
large fruit much duller.

Oak and the Ash,
grow into young tree
Beech and Holly,
and Hornbeam agree,

Fill the hedge with
fruit nuts and berries,
Beech and Hazel nuts,
and stored under leaves

Climbers growing
in hedge create cover,
Old mans beard,
and Ivy they soon take over,
Honey suckle and Dog Rose,
lot of colour provide,
Everything combines,
make our English country side.

Countryman

Love thy neighbor, but pull not down thy hedge
John Ray

Chapter 11

I've got a little Breakdown

Drill bits with the edge knocked off,
The saw it hit a nail,
Hammer's got a headache,
And it needs a brand new stale.

   I'm sure that I'm not alone on these scribing's, most folk won't admit to how their workshop looks, and how it is in every day working. It's not untidy, it's in a natural order of priorities state, and you know where everything is (when you can find it) or where it should be. On walking through the workshop if that's possible, you nearly always see thing that are not wanted right now, and see thing that you had been looking for last week, and now turned up. Things like grinding discs are shoved onto a nail driven into the workshop wall, new hacksaw blades and tap washers the same, various sizes of jubilee clips tied in a loop of string on a nail.
   It seems now when I come to look, the higher the nail the more valuable the item, and it goes right down to the size of the nail to match what it's got to hold. Put it like this, if I threw myself high up the wall, it would be impossible to slide slug like down to the floor, not that you can see much of the floor.

Am I exaggerating on all this? (You will never know.

Axle Stand and his Mate Jack

Axle Stand and his mate,
Hydraulic Jack,
Live in the workshop,
right at the back,

When they're called out,
together they work,
Lifting things heavy,
they call it teamwork.

Adjustable Spanner,
he lives hanging on nail,
Expected to fit every nut,
in the box he assail,
He's first responder,
often carried on tractor,
No hammer to hand,
he's used a persuader.

Poor old Hack he looses
teeth from his blade,
Abused and used to cut anything
for what he's not made,
Hack Saw gets hacked off,
thrown on the bench,
Landing on top of him,
a great heavy old wrench.

Open and Ring Spanner,
Siamese twins in the tools,
Kept in a rolled bag,
with pocket like modules,
Twenty of them,
all different sizes,
Clean and in line
should win all the prizes.

Pilar the drill,
stands aloof in the corner,
His own leg to the floor,
and quite a loner,
His energy comes down,
a wire from the switch,
Grips bit in his chuck,
turns quick without glitch.

Ball Pane is Hammer,
comes in a good many sizes,
Large for the blacksmith,
hot metal he teases
Small one that the Mrs. keep's,
in the cupboard draw,
And ones in between,
working all have loud guffaw.

Claw is another member,
of the same clan,
Pull bent nails, blame
the hammer and not man,
Soon break the stale,
when pulled and abused,
Thrown onto the side,
no stale and unused.

We know how it should be
all tidy and straight,
But never got time to
put back all polish its late,
As long as I can walk
up the middle OK,
And find where I chucked it,
neat pile to display.

I've a little breakdown

I've got a little breakdown
and its needs attention now,
Take it to the workshop,
to bodge it up somehow,
Need to clear the work bench,
with scrap its piled high,
Things that needed mending,
I failed but had a try.

Spanners come in sets,
they're spread all round about,
The very one your wanting,
one you conner do without,
Spend all morning searching,
you end up with a wrench
Round the corner off the nut,
then find its on the bench

The metals rusty, flaking off,
got it to weld somehow,
Clean the edge got some gaps,
must be done right now,
Spitter spatter stop and start,
resembles pigeon siht,
Grind it off and fill the holes,
and hope it wunna split.

Drill bits with the edge knocked off,
saw, that hit a nail,
Hammer's got a headache,
it needs a brand new stale,
Screwdriver hit with hammer,
when chisel conna find,
The spirit level lost its bubble,
guess work I'm resigned.

Have a dam good clear up,
and throw the rubbish out,
Then look for where you've
chucked it little bit of spout,
Ventualy it all comes back,
n' builds up on the floor,
Praps a bigger workshop,
cus I conna shut the door.

I'm really tidy in my mind,
but sometimes I forget,
When I'm in a hurry,
and black clouds and rain a threat,
Tools chucked in the workshop
often miss the bench,
It happens all the while,
I stick with a big old wrench.

But on the whole I'm not alone,
but people don't admit,
They pretend to be perfect
spanners back in tool box fit,
A breakdown always happens,
when you least expect it could,
Then back to get the job done,
as quick as ever should.

———————

I visualize things in my mind before I have to do them. It's like having a mental workshop.
Jack Youngblood

Chapter 12

The Wedding Reception

It was late summer when we had had an invitation to the evening reception of a friend of the misses', sisters daughter was getting married (do you follow). We did not know who she was marrying and had not seen the bride since she was six years old. We got suitably togged up with a present in a fancy presentation box and set off. On arrival we realized it was a big wedding with, could be hundred and fifty guests, all dancing a square dance to noticeable Scottish music, some of the lads including the bride groom were in kilts.

We peeped round the door to see if we could see Misses friend, and then we were ushered in by a waitress, who duly parted us from the present we had brought, for it to be add it to all the other presents on a long table on show near the stage. We sat down trying to see who we knew, well that looks a bit like so and so, and that could easily be sister to our friend, it's a good likeness but could not be sure enough to approach the person. The waitress came round with drinks in fancy glasses and pointed out where the refreshment were, but still after over an hour could not see the friend. As happens at weddings the bride's guests do not know any of the bridegroom's relatives and vice versa, so as folk walked by us they naturally thought we belonged to the other side.

After another half hour the waitress came around with more drinks, and we plucked up courage and asked for the bride's mother by surname, only to be told we had been at the wrong wedding. On divulging our embarrassment to the waitress she said do you want your present back, and luckily it was the same one who had parted us from it when we arrived so she knew what to snaffle back from the table in front of all the guests. This was achieved sneakily with a cloth draped over the box and brought to us in the front porch.

Red with embarrassment and sweating from the tension, we headed to another hotel on the other side of town, where there turned out to be no weddings that day at all. We had three hours away from home, been fed and wined at someone's wedding, we never found out who's it was, did not see a sole that we knew. Later we sat in the chairs at home totally exhausted, and had a good laugh at the fact that we had gate crashed a wedding that we had not been invited to, and no one was ever the wiser for knowing who we were.

Plus as a bonus we still got our present back.

PS The wedding had been the day before, and the present was sent on, somewhat late, to the bride's new home.

Marriage. It's like a cultural-handrail. It links folks to the past and guides them to the future.
Diane Frolov and Andrew Schneider

Chapter 13

The Suckler Cows have started Calving

We left the calves with them for most of the winter only weaning them in mid-February, by this time it had pulled the mothers down, so almost all of the herd now looks "poor" or should I say slim.

Well it's that time of year again and the suckler cows have started calving, so far we have had two. Last year we went through a nightmare calving period where almost every other cow wanted assistance and also we lost a cow and a couple of calves during calving.

We had three sets of twins, one twin calf we found dead at three weeks old with a twisted gut. We had not had a cow have twins for almost twenty years, then as they say about London busses three come along all together. Even the older mature and reliable cows were in trouble, I put it down to a different feeding regime.

The only feed they get every winter is round bale silage made off the same meadows that they graze on, made in July, and containing some of the soft rush rushes that are native to meadow pastures.

Over the winter of 2008/09 we thought it would be a good idea to feed a high energy mineral/ molasses lick supplement, you know the one's where they come in a four gallon bucket, just take the lid off and drop it in the field.

In my opinion, this had grown the calf inside the cow and produced the large calves, it also coincided with the change of bull, and at the time, all the blame was put at his door. But on reflection, some of the cows were fatter than we had had them in other years.

So this last backend 2009 when we should be weaning

all the calves, we sorted out the first calf heifers and a few slimmer cows, and weaned their calves. The rest of the cows that were still too fat, we left the calves with them for most of the winter only weaning them in mid-February, by this time it had pulled the mothers down, so almost all of the herd now looks "poor" or should I say slim.

We have always out wintered the cows, none have ever been in a shed other than the first winter as weaned calves. Our herd is almost like a "hefted" herd, as you get in sheep when they know their own mountain pasture and born to that area of grazing. So it is that our cows, they are used to the peaty meadows that are dissected with bottomless drainage ditches, they get used to the ditches as calves and know it's not a good idea to slip in, in fact the odd calf does drop in but never a second time, and nearly always get themselves out. I dread to think of the time when someone else will bring a new set of cattle to graze down there, and the months they will have of dragging cows or cattle out of ditches, until all have learned their lesson.

On the other hand, when I retire, the wise new comer could or would or should buy my "hefted" cows off me and continue the meadow grazing in a safe and reliable manner.

Signs of Spring

Signs of spring are starting to show,
Though on the hill tops forecast snow,
Bright sunshine warms the sodden ground,
Cold showers and hail still abound.

Lawns and fields look brighter green,
Daffodils open and trumpets beam,
Grass it grows on lawn and verge,
Not on the fields, for the stock to purge,

Birds in hedgerow look to build nests,
Leaf buds appear as if by request,
First eggs are laid soon to be sat,
Full cover of new leaves, hides them thereat.

Badgers are trailing litter to nest,
Digging and cleaning for breeding quest,
Rarely seen but they root for worms,
Under hedgerows and cow pats presence confirms.

Soil it warms in the suns rays,
Germinate seeds dormant upraised,
Soon the countryside transformed and fresh,
Everything growing and looking its best.

If we had no winter, the spring would not be so pleasant: If we did not sometimes taste adversity, prosperity would not be so welcome.
Anne Bradstreet (1612-1672)

Chapter 14

Memories of Olden Days

Memories of olden days,
back then when I were a lad,
Of things we did and said and learnt,
copied from me dad,
Of learning how to talk and walk,
manners got to learn,
Tell the truth and honest be,
respect you've got to earn.

Never cheek your elders,
and address them with respect,
Speak only when you're spoken to,
answer them direct,
Muttering and Laughing,
in your hand it is the worst,
Hold it back don't let it out,
even if you fit to burst.

He taught us how to use his tools,
how to work real hard,
How to earn an honest crust,
In workshop across the yard, make things
useful on the farm, repair them if they broke,
Keep the place all tidy,
he was a very fussy bloke.

He taught us how to plant seeds,
in garden and the fields,
And as they grow look after them
grow to give good yields

Harvest time to bring it in,
and store for winter use,
To feed the family, feed the stock,
to run out's no excuse.

To rear the calves pigs and hens,
and feed them every day,
Milk the cows and collect the eggs,
and sell without delay,
Pigs to take to bacon weight,
and sows to get in pig,
And start the job all over again,
it's always been that way.

Thinking back orr seventy years,
the basic things the same,
Treat others how, you 'd like,
others to treat you the aim,
Manners make'eth man were told,
only yourself to blame,
Rules of life are rules to keep,
it's always been the same.

Time and Tide waits for no man".

    Time is ticking by, time that will not be repeated, were not living life as a rehearsal, we live life now, this minuet, this hour, this day, this week, this month, this year. Time is one of those things that when it is passed, it is gone forever, then, it becomes history. There are people who think they can look into the future and make predictions on what is to come, but decision are often made reflecting on past performance and hope to improve and expand on that.

New inventions alter the way things are done, but no one can invent extra time. The seasons stay the same, and in the same order, plants are geared to the annual germination, growth, flower and seed cycle, as are many of the animals of our planet. A lifetime is pulled down to years, and years to seasons and months, months to weeks, weeks to days, days to hours , hours to minuets, right down to the ticking of the hall clock, and once it's passed, it's gone.

Land is the same, no one can expand the land in this world, the more land that is put under concrete, and the less land there is to sustain the livestock and people of the world. Food is the balancing factor that, when it is in short supply it automatically culls those that rely on it, be it garden birds surviving the winter, or the human population not able to feed itself. No food, equals no life.
It has always been the same over millions of years, the World and everyone on it has to be in balance, and we as humans now have the ability to upset that balance.

The leaders of the countries around the world all end up sooner or later getting things out of balance, be it war or the economy or even wage levels of those who produce nothing to help sustain, or maintain the health or wealth of the world. Each generation has its own go at getting thing right, and each generation starts from what they were brought up to expect. Each generation likes to think they can improve on the life they had as youngsters, but many do not know how to use land and what it's primarily for, and here it's getting into an almighty imbalance.

The day will come and not in my lifetime, where food will again become important enough to be appreciated. Fewer and fewer people alive now will have lived through the last war, with all the rationing that followed for years afterwards. So we must learn from history, and take note of what sustains life. Time is ticking by, time that will not be repeated, were not living life as a rehearsal, we live life now, this minuet, this hour, this day, this week, this month, this year. Make the most of it, as time passes you by more quickly than you realize. Then you turn round and look back and wonder where all that time has gone.

As they say Time and Tide waits for no man.

Time is measured in portions

Time goes by forever,
to history that we can't reset,
Minuets made up seconds,
sixty seconds every minuet,
And hours are made up of minuets,
sixty minutes show,
Days made up of hours,
twenty four in a row,

Week made up of seven days
Monday to Sunday peaks,
A month is one of twelve,
in which it has four weeks,
Spring summer autumn winter,
winter has the snow,
A year it follows the seasons,
four seasons in a row,

A decade that is ten years,
for knowledge to acquire,
A score of years is twenty,
at three score five retire,
A century seems a long time,
for humans to cavort,
Time is measured in portions,
sometimes long or short,
A lifetimes usually shorter,
but it varies quite a lot,
Time on earth it tests you,
before you hit your plot.

Half our life is spent trying to find something to do with the time we have rushed through life trying to save
Will Rogers (1879 - 1935)

Chapter 15

We had a village policeman

We had a village policeman,
and he rode round on his bike,
Quietly ride round lanes and tracks,
to catch a thief and strike,
Early morning late at night,
never knew where he was,
The law he did uphold round here,
and to find the cause.

He lived in the police house,
and it was brand new,
With a lockup cell,
for the criminals he pursue,
Patrolled the parish every day,
on his trusty bike,
Pedaled miles kept him fit,
his flock to him they liked.

Often stopped for a cup of tea,
local news he glean,
Asking who was round about,
and of who we seen,
Strangers snooping, stolen stock,
thing he wants to know,
Its law and order he must keep,
hunt them high and low.

Smugglers of contraband,
of food that's all on ration,
Sold or moved outside the law,
looked and he took action,

A quiet word with farmer friends,
back hander think he got,
Turn a blind eye here and there,
as long as it wasn't shot.

Local poachers, knew them all,
could keep a watchful eye,
He knew the places where to look,
sit and watch and spy,
Catch them red handed on the spot,
take them to his lockup,
Question who and where and when,
the others to round up.

To get around much quicker,
he had a motor bike,
It was a Vesper Scooter,
no longer he catlike,
Could hear him coming,
along the road way back,
His cover blown fore he gets near,
for this we gave him flack.

A panda car, that was next,
to keep him dry and warm
Take on parishes more than one,
for miles away he's drawn,
His cover stretched too far and wide,
not seen about so much,
Of calling on the local folk,
he was out of touch.

The local station that was closed,
from town they had to come,
Call them on the telephone,
so remote they had become,

Every time, a different one,
we didn't know who he was,
They didn't know the area; they
could have come from OZ.

So bring back the local bobby,
give him back his beat,
Get to know the local folk,
and walk and get sore feet,
Know the villages round about,
woods and tracks and lanes,
Were all behind him, bring him back,
the local folk campaign.

The Old Police House Great Bridgeford

The problem with any unwritten law is that you don't know where to go to erase it.
Glaser and Way

Chapter16

Self Sufficiency

In my Fathers years of farming, there was the great depression of the nineteen thirties followed by World War II, which concentrated the government's minds on farming and food production. In my years following the war and rationing farming was appreciated and was treated with importance. But now our country has once again got into the habit of importing ever increasing amounts of what the country needs to feed its inhabitants, and once again gone into a great (financial) depression. (2010 / 2013)

A great majority of people do not give food, or food production any thought and is almost taken for granted. Just a hint of shortage creates a panic by government and individuals as to where they can buy to make up the deficit. But when it is a world shortage and nowhere to buy it from, then food prices shoot up.

Houses built before and for some years after the second world war, had sufficient garden to grow a proportion their own food, Then the pressure was on to build more new houses, and on a given area of land they were crammed closer together, in towns and cities they had the high rise flats. Allotments all over the country have suddenly been revived there being a waiting list in many places to get one. This is where folk who have no garden other than a square of lawn, can go and cultivate an area of ground on which to grow food or anything they like, (more often used just to get away from her in doors).

People these days seem totally incapable of being self-sufficient, no matter how much they grow at home or on the allotment. I remember father telling us that it took a war to bring the country to realize why they have farmers, and much later towards the end of his life, he harked back to it again, hearing us younger generation moaning about making ends meet and paying more and more wages to less and less men on the farm.

Food Miles

On looking back when I were young,
all them years ago,
The horse and cart were still about,
a lot we didn't know,
Cars and tractors taking over,
plenty of fuel they sup,
Fuel brought in from overseas,
and local garages set up.

This has snowballed over the years,
cannot comprehend,
Where all the traffic's going to,
so fast around the bend,
Miles per gallon's going up,
so is car's per mile,
Speed is what's on most people's mind,
then end up in a pile.

Everything is carried about,
and often back again,
Out to distribution centre's,
finding jobs for men,

Wear and tear on tyres and roads,
burning up the miles,
Costs all added onto their goods,
customer pays up and smiles.

At one time, veg came out the ground,
flour came from the mill,
Chickens walked about the yard,
pecking happily to get their fill,
A pig was fattened on scraps,
from the house and garden,
Talk food miles, it was food yards,
when things were all on ration.

Only thing that Mother bought,
was cornflakes in a packet,
Then tins of peaches she would buy,
rom other side the planet,
Had these when bottled fruit ran out,
ate with bread and butter,
Wheat was ground at water mill,
bread baked next to the butcher.

Packaging's the thing right now,
it's wrapped and wrapped again,
Keep the food clean and fresh,
or that is what they claim,
Bin through many hands,
and machines to wrap and pack,
Getting older by the minute,
a use-by date on pack will slap.

Where do you put all the waste produced?
Pop it in the bin,
Land fill holes are filling up,
rotting down n' methane begin,

It all boils down to negligence,
in what were doing to our earth,
How it's changing for the worse,
all getting bigger round the girth.

On looking where it's going to,
well beyond my years,
Food's way down the list to buy,
as" farmers" get the jeers,
Bring it all in from abroad,
more transport still is needed,
"Look after those who tend our land",
make sure the warnings heeded.

There is no love sincerer than the love of food
George Bernard Shaw (1856-1950)

Chapter 17

I had an encounter with an A10 Tank Buster

A few years ago, while ploughing in one of our furthest field, I had an encounter with an A10 Tank Buster, or should I say three of them.
It was the time of the Gulf War, and some American war planes were on training exercise in the UK before being sent on duty giving air cover the troops out in the Gulf.

Each day around mid-morning three of these aircraft came over at high speed at around a thousand feet, banking and turning so as not to fly directly over outlying villages or towns. They were like nothing I had ever seen before, being a very distinctive shape and outline, it had twin fins one at each end of the rear wing, and two engines saddle bag fashion half way along the fuselage. They followed each other perhaps a half mile apart, the sudden noise from the first one, particularly if I was driving or looking the other way, it was enough to frighten anyone, then I knew to expect the next, and the third one.

It was the third day when I was working in that same field when I noticed them coming in the distance over the horizon, approaching very rapidly, then when about a mile or so away I realized that they were flying directly at me. Not over me, not round or down on side or the other, but directly at the tractor. In my mind they had locked their radar, or sights, and aiming at me in the tractor as if it were an enemy tank. I stopped the tractor and in effect froze; it was no use me weaving at three miles an hour to avoid the rockets which could have been deployed in those last seconds. Then when about quarter mile away the pilot must have pulled back on his stick and swooping up from lower than normal, passed directly over the tractor, the following two did exactly the same. It must have given them great satisfaction to have had a "sitting duck" part way through their maneuvers on which they could practice.

It left me sitting in the cab shaking like a jelly, and could not believe what I had witnessed; what with the noise of the jets overhead and what might have happened if one of them had actually produced a friendly fire incident. On the main news that night it reported that A10's were being deployed to the Gulf from their base in Britain. The exercises had taken place for a whole week then all of those aircraft must have flown off on their mission abroad. I have not ever seen another one of those aircraft since other than on the news programs, so if I in my small way had helped those pilots, good luck to them, they will never know me and I will never know them, but I thank them for keeping their fingers off those triggers, and left me to go home for my dinner, shaken but safe.

You can discover what your enemy fears most by observing the means he uses to frighten you.
Eric Hoffer (1902-1983)

Chapter 18

People and Families Born in this House.

Going back 150 years, if walls could talk. In twenty two years the family had eighteen children. It's always a mystery how people lived years ago, particularly in the house that you live in. Our house in its present form was built around the first half of the 1800's. But there is evidence of a previous house. It must have been taken down to door top height (or did it burn down around then) as it has narrow two and half inch bricks on some of the outside walls, then when a larger foot print built it was with larger standard three inch bricks. When the house was extended, the "new" back kitchen where the washing and laundry was done, it was built over the old well, a well that served both the house and the farm and livestock. In dry summers it ran dry and another well was dug in the 1930's deeper about five yards just outside of the house.

Under the floor boards of the older section we found they were supported on fir poles cut directly from the local spinney, cut to length and dropped in place with all the bark still on. The same up in the roof void, the joists and the purlins are 'bark on' fir poles, then in one fairly long room where the joists wanted supporting half way along there is a pair of old bowed ships timbers part of which are exposed in the bedroom, these are of very old and very hard oak still with the evidence of sawn and chopped out joints with peg holes for fixing. These are likely to be part of the old timber frame from the previous house.

The family who I took over from had lived in the village for three generations, starting with William F----

-e born in 1828, he did not marry until he was in his midthirties, his wife being some fourteen years younger. Over the next twenty two years they had eighteen children. William, Edward, Ann & Mary twins, Cecily, Earnest The seventh child Charles (1872) was the one who took over the farm at the age of twenty three when his father died in 1895, then Ellen, John, Walter, William, Horace, Florence, Arthur, Eleanor, Dora, Arnold, and last one Frank. One of the lads from this eighteen, eventually became a notable judge in the law courts of London, some went out farming to South Africa, and others spread out all over the world to make their fortune.

Over the years that we have lived here, we have had overseas visitors/relatives who are descendants of William (1828) wanting to look round the old house, and look where and how their grandparents lived and how they were brought up. I know the family had a reunion a few years ago, with family members flying in from South Africa, Australia and all point of the globe, with, in the region of a hundred members turning up. On the family tree that I have to hand drawn up in 2009 by a descendant living in the north of England, a retired vet, there are over four hundred names of relatives stemming from William at this house and farm, it is thought that there are still some of whom have not traced.

As I said the seventh child Charles (1872) took over the Farm on his father's death and eventually married and they had five children. Marion who worked in the house and no one ever saw her, Ruth who worked in the farm dairy cleaning the dairy utensils, but if anyone came in the yard she would scurry round the back way and back into the house, Earnest who eventually took over the farm in the 1950's when his father died, and Frank who did go in the air force during the war, then worked on the farm, and Margaret who worked at the milking and rearing the calves, it was said the she did have an admirer at one stage in her younger days, but he was sent packing when her mother judged him to be "not good enough" for her. None of these five ever married and so there were no grandchildren for Charles (1872).

Earnest was trained as a chemist in his younger days and then came back to the farm taking over from his father and stayed tenant until 1983 when he retired due to ill health that is when I moved here and took the tenancy. One interesting item we found in the garden was a huge pestle and mortar, we think it must have been the property of Earnest, it was in good condition and would hold I would think two gallons in capacity, the mortar was made of turned elm wood and starting to decay with age, but the stone/marble mortar or whatever its made of is as new and stand high on a shelf in our kitchen weighing a good quarter of a hundred weight (13.5 kg to them's who need to know).

Their mother Elizabeth, Charles's wife, was very dominating; the children went to school next door but were not allowed to play with the other village children. At play times, at school next door, every day, mornings and afternoons they had to return to their own front gate and wait for the bell to go, before returning to their studies. The children never got to handle money, and had not got any grasp of its value until their parents died. That was when the brothers started to buy machinery, after a short while they bought a David Brown Cropmaster tractor which had two seats so the brothers could work it together. Then they went on to have two tractors both Ferguson Massy 35's, one each, and the matching equipment. The biggest snag for them was that they had no idea of maintaining or repairing machines, all repairs and adjustments were made by the local machinery dealers, they being more stock men.

One of Earnest's early purchases was a bunch of very fine Hereford cross steers for fattening off on grass, he had not been used to bidding at market and his excitement of the day, which was quickly picked up by the auctioneer and the seller of the cattle, he paid well over the odds. When the same bunch were sold some twelve months later they fetched less than when he had bought them. This trend of not knowing the value of money dogged them all the years the brothers farmed.

The same went for the three sisters, it was said that they went into a milliners in town on what must have been their first ever shopping spree free from their mother's domination, and bought five splendid hats each. Not for any special occasion as they never ventured out very often, but just to feel the power of spending money.

The eldest daughter lived in her bedroom for the last twenty years of her life, no one in the village had seen her in all those years. The second daughter worked hard in the house and dairy and fell down the back stairs and broke bones, being old she had never been away from the house and was admitted to hospital, the shock of other people working round and on her killed her. The last sister and two brothers were not able to continue farming, as age was against them and they retired to a house in the next village. Margaret died partly from the stress over the previous few years, and partly from not being able to cope with a small house, the furniture they took with them filled the house as if it were warehouse and they could not move around. The two brothers could not cope on their own and went into a rest home together.

This did not last long as they kept falling out, and one of them moved to another home, they visited each other on a regular basis when they too died after some years in care.

Other things may change us, but we start and end with family.
Anthony Brandt

Chapter19

It happened one fine summer afternoon

It happened one fine summer afternoon, when I went to bring the cows in for milking, they all get strung out when the cows decide, as usual, to all walk single file over the foot bridge over the ford in the back lane. To make the job slower, some of them stop to rub an itch on their nose on the bridge side rails.

Very few liked to walk through the ford itself because of the round cobbles stones in the bottom.

They turn into the farmyard off the lane between the farm house and the double cowshed where they would normally amble through the doors and find their own stalls. But on this one day each cow that went through the gate stumbled onto their knees, scramble back onto their feet and panicked and fled down to the far end of the yard.

It affected some cows worse than others, and with

them arriving all spread out in single file from around a corner it caught each one by surprise. Not knowing what was happening way back at the rear of the herd I realize something was wrong when the last of the cows in front of me collapsed then scrambled with hooves slipping on the concrete and race off to the others standing startled in the far corner of the farm yard.

As I walked through the gate I too felt a tingle through my boots, a shock, a currant of electricity, my feet had boots on that part insulated me from what all the cows had just experienced, it was quite clear it was not going to be a normal pleasant afternoons milking.

We investigated what could be making the yard "live", but it came inconclusive, we turned all mains electric boxes to the off position, but still the yard was "live", so the Midlands Electricity Board (MEB) was called. It was a mystery to them at first, as they found nothing amiss on our premises. They started to follow the main wires out to the first pole out on the roadside, then up to the next farm, then to a group of cottages, at each stage they disconnected and re-connected to eliminate them as the cause of the leakage.

The village school connection then another farm, then the blacksmiths shop, then on to the village pub. Here they found that electricity was being fed down the neutral wire for some reason and on down to our cowsheds and running to earth through our earth wires, which in turn was clipped to the underground water pipes leading from the house to the cowsheds. Once the pub was disconnected from the mains everything returned to normal, and we had the job of coaxing the cows back up the yard and into the shed to be tied up. We were some two or three hours late milking that day, and the cows had had time to calm down and stood chewing their cud wandering why they had not been milked.

On deeper investigation it turned out that the publican had just bought himself a new second hand cooker that he had wired in himself, and made the wrong connections when he installed it. I have no doubt that the MEB would have had a few sharp words to say to him, and the danger he had posed to other villagers and livestock.

Had the connection been made an hour or so later, when all the cows would have been tied in the shed by metal chains, to metal stalls, attached to metal water pipes, connected to all the water bowls, it could have killed the lot. It seems that as low as thirty or forty volts will kill a cow, whereas us with wearing boot or wellingtons and we have the ability to run out of the sheds are more likely to have survived the situation.

I was surprised the following day to hear back from someone who was in the pub that night how the publican was laughing and bragging how he had nearly killed off a herd of cows when he turn on his cooker, fried beef and all that, but then I suppose it made a good talking point at the bar for quite a while, but it was no laughing matter at the time for us, it was before the time when earth trips were invented and became compulsory. Electricity is an invisible killer.

Faith is like electricity. You can't see it, but you can see the light.   Author Unknown

Chapter 20

The Dentist

This is a copy of a letter/email to a friend of mine down the road who is recovering at home from a serious operation.

Dear John,
As you may have gathered, we haven't got much on at the moment, and a bit of time to bgguer about writing. As you must know when I had my op on my knees they for some mysterious reason they insisted I see a dentist, somatt ta do with a rotten tooth could make the metal in the joint reject. But John you must have been told this for what op's you've been throooo.
Before my op, I had never in me life sat in a dentist chair, or had anyone fiddle with me teeth, so I booked in at Castlefields Surgery dentist, pay a monthly standing order ca-chinnnnnnng, (their cash till) , and pay them a visit every six months. I have been there now twenty times in the last ten years and still they have done nothing other than scrape and polish. I have cleaned (brushed is what they call it) my teeth once before each visit on the morning of the visit (Nothing to be proud of according to Eileen, but then I call it sour grapes as she cleans her teeth two time a day every day and almost always has to have something done (ca---chinnnnnnng) So I am getting to know my dentist quite well, for they know they only have to count them and poke round them, and find time to fill in the ten minuet slot allotted to me. She asked me (the dentist), as I think they are asking every customer, what is my experience or my views while in the dentists. (She will wish she hadn't).

So John I closed my eyes and this is what I envisaged.

Are you Sitting Comfortably?

Sit looking through dark goggles,
up into a light,
Shining from a wobbly arm,
just a tad off white,
Hovering just above ya head,
no sun tan will you get,
Just a beam of light to shine,
think it's my sunset.

A two inch square to tissue,
n' a cup weak bilberry juice,
Open up me north and south,
now there's no excuse,
They always seem to work behind,
where you cannot see,
And speak in muffled tones aloud,
casual and carefree.

The high-tech chair jumps down a step,
head below me feet,
A clink of tools are gathered up,
dentist adjusts her seat
Forelocked head of curls appear,
eyes behind a shield,
A tool gripped in big knuckled fingers,
now begin to wield.

A rear view mirror push down me throat,
see my teeth all round,
Couple of inches further down,
me tonsils will be crowned,

Only counting what I've got,
choking on me tongue,
Call themselves a dentist,
hope they won't take long.

A hook appears before my eyes,
gripped tight in dentist's fist,
"Open wide and move ya tongue,
see what's on my checklist",
Hoover pipe switched on too high,
clean me mouth outright,
Wonder what's found in the bag,
when they clean it out at night.

The foundation of each tooth is cleaned,
n' fertilize the roots,
With gritty paste they brush right in,
just like cleaning boots,
Reared back up in jerky chair,
feet back on the floor,
Blood runs back into me toes,
me bulging eyes back in once more.

They've no idea what we go through,
the trauma and the stress,
Quaking in our shoes they ask,
have we got your right address,
Your medication up to date,
just got to tick the box,
N' sign it at the bottom,
"Oh I see you've had small pox".

New appointment six months time,
ring you day before,
Make sure were live and kickin,
and brushed me teeth once more,

Got to have them checked again,
keep the rot at bay,
A healthy head of teeth's the aim,
is what I should portray.

I'd Hate to Upset my Dentist

I'd hate to upset my dentist,
the revenge they could inflict,
You cannot see their face at all,
but their eyes you can depict,
A knee upon my chest to hold,
me down while they inject,
Now I know what mole grips are,
from my tool box nicked,

To grip and pull and twist with glee,
a sound tooth they would eject,
With pain and blood and sweat and tears,
I know that I've been tricked,
Touch of a button on the chair,
and upright I am flicked,
To sway and stumble for my coat,
this I should predict,

Tooth ache still there I am aware,
no strength have I object,
May be better next time round,
think this was why I panicked.
I wake up from my nightmare;
on the calendar I've ticked,
When next to see the dentist,
their appointment time is strict,

"Be here at ten, you know the rules",
then with her finger clicked,
Computers will not bend the time,
and cannot be unpicked,
So to Nicola and her crew I beg,
your boots they will be licked,
I will tell all those I know,
you are the best in this district,
And please don't bare a grudge with me,
my age it does restrict,
I'm old and grey, come what may,
so please let's change this subject.

———————

All the best to you John,

Fred

PS. By the way we will be ploughing down by you in a few weeks' time

Dentist, n.: **A Prestidigitator who, putting metal in one's mouth, pulls coins out of one's pocket.
Ambrose Bierce (1842-1914)**

Chapter 21

Irreversible Changes in one Small Village

As in all small villages it changes over the years, in some way for the better, in others for the worse. The village pumps went some fifty years ago, these were a meeting point for gossip, and news was soon spread from end to end of the village.

The school on the other hand has expanded, the frontage is as it was in years gone by, but round the back a complete new complex of class rooms has been developed.

The blacksmiths shop closed with decline in the Shire horse population and tractors took over the heavy work about the farms.

The village wheelwright's work shop closed when the wheelwright retired, which coincided with the metal hydraulic tipping trailers and the popularity of the light metal gates and wheel barrows. The coffin making gradually ceased when the in town undertakers took over with the motor hearse. In the early days the hearse was a four wheel trolley housed behind the church, and the wheelwright took the coffin on the hearse on foot to the house or cottage. For the later years I remember he worked with one of the town undertakers, he made the coffin and dug the grave, they did the transport, just another craftsman and his trade has disappeared from the village.

The village pub has survived up until recently when it closed for some months at the end of 2009. It has been hit by the recession along with a lot of other country pubs, it now opened again, and seems to be bumping along, and surviving.

It is hoped that it will pull through as it will take the heart out of the village if it closes for good. At least it's not being demolished.

The post office shop closed some years ago when the GPO decide to do away with many rural post offices, that again is or was right in the middle of the village, the shop itself went into decline with the rise of super markets and the improvement of transport, nearly every household has at least one car. The postman used to come on his bike four miles from the sorting office to deliver mail and parcels, that changed over to a van a long time ago, in fact some forty years it's been delivered by van.

The farms have reduced, ours is the only one left in the centre of the village, and four other "in the village" farms have been amalgamated with the surrounding farms. Where at one time all the cottages had farm workers in them as they were all tied cottages to the different farms. Now nearly all the cottages have been sold off or let to folk who work outside of the village.

The church itself has not changed but the vicars job is now spread over three other village churches, spreading his message to a greater number of people over a wider area.

A Country Village (1950's)

The Village has its own clock,
for to tell the time,
On the tower of St Chads,
every half hour it does chime,
This its done for many years,
and to wind it up you climb,
Three big weights on cables,
crank it many times.

In the tower set in oak frame,
sit its ringing bells,
Ropes and wheels for swinging,
its congregation tells,
Come to church for service,
to have your sins expelled,
All the parish can hear them,
peal of Village bells.

The vicar has his job to visit,
all parish elderly and the sick,
Take all the Sunday services,
with sermon long and epic,
Christmas Easter Harvest,
Christenings funerals and weddings quick,
He is kept so busy looking after,
all village elderly and sick.

Out and down the church path ,
s the village green,
Under the lynch gates,
standing all serene,
Looks a little weathered,
for all the years its been,
Guarding the church yard,
on the village green.

Also on Village green,
was the village pump,
Standing in the corner,
on a grassy hump,
To prime it work the handle,
almost had to jump,
Water all the cottages,
from this well and pump.

Across the road to educate,
is the village school,
Teacher at the blackboard,
sitting on a stool,
There to help the children
not to be a fool,
Basic reading writing,
maths in the village school.

Further down the village,
was the blacksmiths shop,
Making all the horse shoes,
on the anvil hot,
Hammer always ringing,
shaping metal without stop,
Give the horses new shoes,
to make them clip and clop.

Next again is Holly Bush,
our local village pub,
As well as drink you can get if hungry,
a little bit of grub,
For a gathering of the locals,
this was the hub,
News and gossip turned around
in the village pub.

Undertaker in the village,
was at the wheelwrights shop,
Lays out and measures them,
made a coffin non-stop,
Family lines the coffin,
his brother dug the grave,
All the week they made farm carts,
spokes whittle to a stave.

Down at the post office,
in the village shop,
Sells all essentials,
also chocolate sweets and pop,
Letters parcels postal orders,
have a hefty whop,
Rubber stamp saying Seighford,
in the village shop.

The Village Shop and Post Office

The postman came on his bike to visit,
six days of every week,
Delivering post and parcels,
each morning his bike it creaked,
Collecting all the gossip while,
having cup of tea he'd speak,
All about what he'd learned,
on his round six days every week.

On all the farms they had cows,
and they produce the milk,
Beef and chickens hens and geese,
sheep with fleece smooth as silk.
They had mixture of everything,
corn for cows and pigs,
Hay and roots, rolled oats and peas,
feed the cows produce the milk,

In all the cottages were the families,
men who work the land,
Herdsmen, n' wagoner's,
n' those to anything can turn their hand,
Early start in all weathers,
generally a happy band,
They work late at harvest time,
all these men who work the land.

A sense of curiosity is nature's original school of education.
Dr. Smiley Blanton.

Cottages and the pump demolished around 1950

The old village pump was situated between this pair of cottages and the shop (west side of the shop) picture dated around the 1890's.

A House is no home unless it contains food and fire for the mind as well as the body.
Margaret Fuller (1810 - 1850)

Chapter 22

Up to now we haven't had a Drop (rain)

This was written on 15th July 2010 which was a very dry spring and summer

Me cows are out on grass,
and the pastures burning up,
The brook is running low,
soon be nothing left to sup,
They're roaming round the fields,
n' pulling at the hedge,
Even eating at the rushes,
and they're pulling at the sedge.

No grass to cut for aftermath,
hasn't grown an inch,
And the corn is short and stunted,
two tons an acre at a pinch,
Straw is short and brittle,
come through combine just like dust,
Need a baler like a Hoover,
suck it off the old earth's crust.

Feed for winter not enough,
and the bedding it's the same,
It's the climate that is changing,
and the weather is to blame,
When the weather breaks at last,
n' it won't know when to stop,
Flooding and the rain,
up to now we haven't had a drop.

———————

Chapter 23

Mother made her Pastry (1940's)

I would like to bet there are not many women these days that make pastry every week like our mother did, and in the volume now only seen in a super market bakery, *(I am exaggerating a bit)*. But with seven of us in the farm house to cater for at that time, and just when we were growing up, she showed us how to cook and bake cakes, and of course make pastry.

Mother made her Pastry

Mother made her pastry,
mixed in a great mixing big bowl,
Then thumped it on the table,
with the rolling pin she'd roll,
Used all sorts to cut the rings,
no proper cutter got,
A glass or cup or old pan lid,
something just right size she'd spot.

Jam tarts large with fancy edge,
jam tarts small and neat,
Mince pies filled with lid on top,
all look too good to eat,
Spare pastry given to us kids,
to roll and make our own,
Rolling out and cutting pastry,
just like we'd been shown.

It went grey in our hands,
our hand got cleaner too,
Currant flap-over sealed down,
whipped egg brushed on for glue,

Then we used the pastry tins,
greased the inside more,
So they'd pop out without sticking,
as mother did before.

Should go on the cooling rack,
but ours were not there long,
Eaten soon as cool enough,
so as not to burn our tongue,
No crumbs left of what we made,
and mothers dare not touch,
Cooled and stored in an air tight tin,
to last a week's too much.

———————

A cold need the cook as much as the doctor.
Scottish Proverb

Chapter 24

Fields lanes and Country Roads all have Names

Our Village is a small part of England, as say a motor car is made up of component parts. The largest being the body, the chassis, the engine, right down to the smallest bolt washer and cotter pin.

So Great Britain is made up of England, Scotland and Wales, these are again divided into counties, cities, towns, villages and hamlets and this continues down into individual house names. Where you have Motorways, trunk roads, main roads, secondary roads, by roads, country roads, and village roads. As in all areas of the country side - it continues into farm roads and lanes. Round our village, starting with the Back lane, you go then into the Moor Lane, which runs north to the railway line and the Flash Bridge. (Railway Bridge) Off this lane runs the Love Lane to the north of the village, coming back onto the Bridgeford road below Cooksland House. On the east side, we have got the Moss Lane, this runs to the Ashes Wood. Then to the south east the Oldfords Lane, that runs through to Coton-Clanford.
To the south side, we have Smithy Lane, a cow track for the Village Farm cows to go to pasture, and a public footpath. Finally on the west side Clanford Lane (This last one is a council road), leading as it says to Coton-Clanford.

Off all these lanes are fields, the majority of which are named. These would be well known among the people of the village, as nearly all would work on the farms. But nowadays there are very few farm workers, and the vast majority commute to work elsewhere. Some have logic as to how they were named; in fact all must have at some point.

Take the Red Reins for instance, this is a field when ploughed, it turns up in heavy red clay, and when all the ploughing had to be done in "Cop and Rein". (You set a cop with the plough and plough both sides of it. When it meets the previous cop further across the field this is called a Rein where you finish off the ploughing in between). Then you have a field called Hobble End, which used to have a double cottage in it with no services whatever. There only remains a pipe in the hedge which reveals the proximity of the well. There are also the remains of the garden wicket in the hedgerow, this was Hobble End Cottages.

Other names need more and deeper investigation, such as Noon's Birch, Hazel Graze, Big Ashpit, Middle Ashpit, Little Ashpit, the Fosters, and the Pingles, Mill Bank, Hanging Bank (this one makes you think!), The Cumbers the row of houses were named after the grass fields behind them. There is also Moss Common, Passage Field and, Glebe Field. There are a lot of small fields about that are Glebe land and were part of the farm attached to the Church, the old vicarage had a cowshed. We have the Stafford Meadow, the Shed Meadow, and an archaeological dig or even ploughing the old turf up might reveal the remains of a building on this field. The Public field is on the bank behind the Holly Bush pub. The pub had fields attached to it and the small range of buildings on the east side of the pub car park were the cowsheds to it, which included a coach house for the Trap, a stable, a loose box for young stock or pigs and, a loft with a pitching hole where the hay was pitched in, The cowshed is still in the same format as it was a hundred years ago with the old wooden stalls the lot. You step back in a time warp when you go in there.

This has only scratched the surface of the history of

the village, and much more can be found out depending on where you look at it from. Everyone has a different stand point.

This pattern is repeated all over the country, very little is known by the general public that almost all fields up and down the country have names, some more interesting than others, as with house names it makes life more interesting than just a number.

**Mid pleasures and palaces though we may roam,
Be it ever so humble, there's no place like home.**

John Howard Payne (1791 – 1852)

Chapter 25

Black Gold

This was written a few weeks ago before the wheat prices "took off", I have no doubt that very little wheat will find its way to the power stations this year. (Autumn 2010) In case you are looking at this in years to come, its the year when Russia had wild fires and very dry season, and burned large areas of standing wheat.

Black Gold

At great expense they drill for oil,
Black gold to be refined
Wells are sunk beneath the earth,
Through rock and soil grind,
Pumped and piped on its way,
Into many products turned,
Ammonium nitrate, tar and pitch,
Petrol diesel, n' heating oil burned.

It's running out and hard to find,
Now digging neath the waves,
Risks are getting higher,
As for greater profit craves,
Barrel price keeps going up,
And at the pumps the same,
There's plenty more where that comes from, Or that is what they claim

Biofuels the thing right now,
Grown on our land and earth,
Each season brings a new crop,

To feed it now not worth,
Another market for our wheat,
No surplus stores we need,
Persuade the millers pay the price,
And end the waste and greed.

Energy from wind power,
Great turbines in the sky,
Out upon the hill tops,
No wind no power supply.
Tide and wave power harness now,
Reliable as can be,
Clean and safe, its ebb and flow,
The energy is free.

———

Our own season was quite dry and reduced the straw length, which saw straw prices on the field in the swath go through the roof with £60 and £70 per acre not uncommon with odd fields higher a lot than that

The oil well in the Gulf of Mexico has now been plugged, and most of the slick has dispersed, even that disaster will pale into the background, and soon be forgotten.

Oil prices have fallen lately. We include this news for the benefit of gas stations, which otherwise wouldn't learn of it for six months.

Bill Tammeus, *in Toronto's National Newspaper, 1991*

Chapter 26

The Longest Swath

British Food Packed not Grown

Food comes in around the globe,
then packed and labeled here,
All put into bubble packs,
then Britain gets a cheer,
Stick on the labels, printed here,
a union jack the lot,
It's only the packaging,
but the contents they are not.

Packaging's the thing right now,
it's wrapped and wrapped again,
Keep the food clean and fresh,
or that is what they claim,
Bin through many hands,
and machines to wrap and pack,
Getting older by the minute,
a use-by date on pack will slap.

Everything is carried about
and often back again,
Out to distribution centre's,
finding jobs for men,
Wear and tear on tyres and roads,
burning up the miles,
Costs all added onto their goods,
customer pays up and smiles.

British food grown and packed,
genuine through and through,
A clear label telling us,
so we know on what we chew,
Local grown just down the road,
fresh as the morning dew,
We need to know, it's only fair,
right now we haven't a clue.

The Longest Swath

    I seem to walk and work about the farm these days in a reflective daze, half looking back, and half looking forward, with everything starting to overtake my way of working. I look at the trees and hedges some of which I planted over my life on the farm, and how we used to mow and plough right up to the edge of every field. After all the longest swath or the longest furrow is always the one round the outside of the field. We cut the hedge banks by hand and trimmed the lower branches of young hedge row trees and trimmed the hedges with a brushing hook.
    Looking now we don't have the same labour force, but is it so hard to cut that last back swath of hay/silage right up to the ditch or plough that last furrow and plough out the corners properly. They have the excuse now that it's for the wildlife, but back then we had far more wildlife than we have now, or so it seemed. I see the balance of the countryside gradually changing over the years, and reflect on what it looked like sixty years ago, but then memories can be selective.
    When growing up everything around you is the "norm", you take it all for granted that that is how thing

have always been, when in reality, your parents and grandparents went through or have gone through modernization and change over their years. The situation we have today in farming and the world of farming in general is just the "norm" for all those starting up a farming operation now. It's all I suppose what they call progress

I don't think my father had an overdraft in his life, what he bought he saved up for, worried for days if his cash flow (the word cash flow is too modern, never heard of it until I went to farm college) was running low. Friday mornings were the crunch day when mother came home from shopping after calling at the bank for the wages for the men, (about twelve pound a man). It was like a big bank roll stuffed deep in her handbag, and quickly transferred when she got home into father's desk and locked up for the night, wages being paid out on a Saturday mornings.

Money had been very tight for my parents in their early days in farming, and they knew how to run a tight ship, nothing was ever spent if it did not need to be spent. There had always got to be a guaranteed return, and this habit never left them in all the years of their life, whether it be the first fertilizers ever purchased onto the farm (nitro-chalk, basic slag, Humber fish muck) or whether it be knitting wool for knitting all our socks gloves and jumpers, which eventually became working garments and were darned and repaired many times before they were too holey to repair. Thrift was the by word then, and we seem to have lost that word from the modern day vocabulary, it's become a throwaway society now, nothing is repaired, if it don't work chuck it, and get a new one. Maybe that's why I still have a couple of old tractors in the shed, still in good working order, but not anywhere near as comfortable as the modern ones, still got an old scythe hanging up and a brushing hook, you never know when you might need them (you silly old Bugger), I probably haven't got the strength now to work them now anyway.

.Mother Always Worked So Hard   (1945)

Mother always worked so hard,
rear her brood of kids,
As we grew bigger and in our teens,
we must have cost her quids,
Four of us lads and our dad,
Uncle Jack as well,
Looked after all of us,
Knitting socks and jumpers she excelled

Rabbit pie most every week, killed a pig and cured,
Only thing she did buy,
big lump of beef well matured.
Bottled all the fruit she could,
and salted down the beans,
Got the meals and baked the cakes,
did washing in between,

Baker came three times a week, six loaves every call,
Corn flakes she also brought,
lot of boxes I recall,
Through the war and rationing,
never seemed go short,
Well fed, we all worked hard,
and not much time cavort.

Nature is the most thrifty thing in the world; she never wastes anything; she undergoes change, but there is no annihilation, the essence remains - matter is eternal.   Horace Binney

Chapter 27

The War time Blackout

The farm I was brought up on during the war is situated about five hundred yards from the end and on the north side of the main runway of a war time airfield, and across to our west side was the perimeter track where the aircraft taxied round to take off. Close by was the petrol dump, where the fuel was delivered by road tankers and collect by refueling vehicles and taken round parked planes. If ever an enemy bomb had made a direct hit, it certainly would have rocked our foundations.

Just along from that was a search light, parked on a large circle of concrete some thirty yards outside the perimeter track. There were a number of woods around the outside of the airfield, and this was where the bomb dumps were built with concrete tracks leading all the way round and back to the perimeter track. The safest way for an enemy bomber to get this far inland was at night, and if they could not find their allotted target, they would circle round looking for lights, or some evidence of a target to unload their bombs. It was important not to present them with a target in the first place, that was why around the farm yard, every cowshed window had to have blinds made for the "blackout" . A wooden frame was made to fit each window and black tarred paper was tacked onto it. All the cowshed doors were kept closed during dark nights while milking was in progress. Only the down stairs windows of the house had these blinds as when you went to bed it was often with a candle and that was only to see your way to bed.

A low voltage generator had been installed at the Beeches Farm house before we moved in, with its wires fastened to the walls with insulators consisting of a pair of porcelain blocks with a hole in the centre for the wood screw and each side of that was grove to take the wire. The two were clamped together holding the wires just off the surface they were fastened to.

When the mains 240 volts came, a transformer was installed by the electricity meter. That meant that for years, while the old wiring was reasonably serviceable, father had to go to a warehouse quite a few miles away (up the Potteries) for replacement 24 volt bulbs.
No such thing as an earth wire with that system, the radio had a two pin plug as did the table lamp and standard lamps, so for a while there was a mixture of new mains and the old wire running round the house, as gradually mother had an electric cooker and an electric iron on a three pin socket.

The mains were taken across the yard to an electric motor that was installed to drive all the barn machinery including the milk vacuum pump, and the existing loft shaft system. The old barn engine with two big flywheels was disposed of, only the block of concrete that it once stood on, with four bolts sticking up, gave evidence as to where it once had pride of place. The electric motor had a pulley each side of it and just occasionally it drove the corn plate mill and the milking vacuum pump at the same time. When the mill finished it was a matter of running the long leather belt off the motor pulley with a bit of wood. The vacuum pump belt reached from one side of the barn to the other across a doorway into the next shed, and during milking times you had to stride over the flapping belt. The mill belt was longer, and the one onto the loft shafting longer still, where it had belts to a chaff cutter, a root pulper, a cake crusher, and at one time a winnower.

Black Molasses in the Barn

I remember at the Beeches, way back in the barn,
Great big forty gallon drum, on block away from harm,
It contained black molasses; a good half of it was used,
With hot water mixed, poured on oats when they were bruised.

Take the bung out and wait a bit, for it to slowly flow,
We all liked to have a taste; dad said it'd help us grow,
A finger full and then another, it was lov-ely and sweet,
Left your hands all sticky, you couldn't be discrete.

We had plenty over the time, but still a lot unused,
Mother said it would move us, father he was amused,
He said a good clean out, every now and then,
Would tone us up, and help us all, to grow to big strong men.

Her own mother lived in her later years of her life in the horrible suspicion that electricity was invisibly dripping all over the house
James Thurber - (1894 – 1961)

As you see this is a picture of a picture, the village church of St. Chads is above the cluster bottom right. Right of centre at the bottom is the village school. Left of centre near the bottom is my farm, the only farm left out of five farms.

Top left at the end of the road is where we were brought up as kids, the home farm. Then two fields to the left out of the top left of the picture is the old airfield, so we were all fairly vulnerable to attack.

Faith is like electricity. You can't see it, but you can see the light.
Author unknown

Chapter 28

I'm Not an Educated Chap

I am not an educated chap, I have difficulty stringing words together to write down, let alone sepllign them correctly, so I find the spell checker on the computer an absolute must.

This is the first writing I have done, since the essays we did at school some sixty years ago. For me it's a one finger job typing, which is about the same speed as my thinking, and as for putting in the full stops and comers, I get short of breath these days, and I am told, every comer is for a pause for breath, hence, the, numerous, c,o,m,e,r,s, . Okay I am over doing it a bit, but you will know what I mean eventually someday, if you don't now.

This picture is from the corner of our house, we are looking across the front lawn, over the trimmed hedge is the road through the village and the other side of that is the village green. The building on the right is the village school where my mother went from the age of three (1910) taught by Miss Pye who and also taught me 35 years later in the same class. My son also went there from the age of four only having literally yards to walk to school.

I Remember Miss Pye

Miss Pye was our teacher, in the infant's class,
Taught all us to write, everyone en mass,
With big bold loops, and Capitals a Flourish,
We all did our best, so as not to be punished.

Mother she taught, To write same way,
Looks like my writing, as I write my essay,
Holding the pen, and biting my lip,
Concentrate on writing, without a slip.

Numbers and tables, we did recite,
Chanting each morning, without respite,
Letters and alphabet, practiced each day,
Till words we could write, then go out to play.

In winter when cold, big coal fire she had,
And pulled up our chairs, when learning to add,
Kind teacher she was, no cane in sight,
Cared for us all, no matter, how dim, the light.

In the "Big" school that we went to at the age of eleven in town, we had wood work and metal work lessons. A whole half day for the whole term, in fact the class was split into two, half the class went woodwork, and half to metalwork, then swapped over at the end of every term (a school term is short of 3 months).
Everyone, that is the pupils, got on well with Harry Nutter in the metal work class, he was kind and patient with those who were not very practical, he guided and helped them and he allowed us who had finished our item, to help those who struggled.

We started by making a round washer, then a square washer, and on to make a brass toasting fork (Toasting forks went out of fashion years ago, I doubt if most of the younger generation now know what one even looks like let alone used one) .Then we made a round copper bowl with a brass bead round the edge and the same round brass rod soldered on to make the base. The copper had to be rubbed with soap then heated until the soap went black, to soften the metal, then it was beaten on a leather pouch filled with sand with a ball pane hammer, this process was repeated until it was deep enough, and the shape that was desired.

We even helped Harry Nutter to cut panels out of his Morris Thousand van, an ex post office van, and helped him fit the glass in the sides. This was done in his lunch hour, and he was glad of a bit of help. Eventually we were shown how to work the lathe, on which I made a tractor drawbar peg complete with a pointed end and a small hole in which to put a retaining clip, a thick washer was brazed round its neck then the handle was shaped and heated and bent across almost 45degrees to form the handle, it lasted for a good many years before it got lost.

The wood work teacher was another matter, he was almost the opposite to Harry Nutter, his name was "Bulldog" Lees, he had a permanent scowl on his face and all the four years at that school I never saw him crack a smile. He did not seem to mix with the other teachers, at break time he would be tatting about his immaculate classroom checking on how sharp his chisels were and touching up the saw blades. (There were twenty of every tool and ten benches with two vices on each) All the tools were arranged in two wide cupboards at the back of the room, so that when the doors were wide open, small tools were in racks on the doors, and larger one's on on the allotted shelves, any tool missing would be spotted before anyone left the classroom. There were no power tools back then, he showed us how to saw without putting pressure on the saw, "if the saw is sharp, its own weight is enough to do the cutting" we were told, and he could soon tell if we had not listened. His response to any deviation from what you were told came in a loud booming deep voice that almost shook the glass in the windows, and anyone who dare to cross him more than once (in a lifetime), he had your card marked for good. Bulldog even demonstrated his anger one day by throwing a chisel, from the front of the classroom into the back of an open store cupboard on the back wall dagger fashion. It was rumored that he had been a sergeant in the army where he trained men hand to hand dagger fighting, and dagger throwing. I can tell you when that happened it frightened all the class ridged, and no one dare even ask a question.

We Had a Woodwork Teacher (1950 ish)

We had a woodwork teacher;
we called him Bulldog Lees,
Had stern face and bad temper,
no one dare to tease,
If he could not get class attention,
throw a chisel hard,
Hit the back wall cupboard,
like a dagger stuck and jarred.

All the class it stood and quivered
dare not cross his path,
The respect was thrust upon you;
dare not stir his wrath,
No one liked his lessons,
even those who could push a plane,
Perfection in this man and all his tools,
but he was a bloody pain.

Natural ability without education has more often attained to glory and virtue than education without natural ability
Cicero (106 BC - 43 BC)

Chapter 29

Loading Cattle

On the odd occasion, now and then, things take a different turn to what you have planned for that day. I had planned to take two big steers in to Market, checked their tags, they had been pre-movement TB tested, filled the entry form and signed the passports. Up early on the morning with the trailer already hooked up to the Land Rover, leaned over the field gate and shouted the bunch of cattle down to the yard where they have been starting to eat some silage. Once in the shed it was a matter of sorting out the two I wanted, and run them into the race. On the end of the race is the cattle crush from where we are able to load cattle directly into the trailer.

Reversed up the trailer with the tailboard right up to the crush gate, pulled in a side yard gate, and opened the trailer side gates. Everything is set with no possibility of escape, a job I done so many time over the years. Opened the race gate for the cattle to move forward through the crush and followed them through the crush tapping them on gently with a stick.

First one walked into the trailer then as the second one walked in, the first one turned and walked back out onto the tailboard, I pulled the crush gate almost too shutting myself safely inside the crush at the same time tapping the head of said bullock who proceeded to turn and go back into the trailer. As he quietly turned and ducked backwards, his rump hit the crush gate, springing the partly open gate shut very rapidly, me with me yed ducked down in the crush got a ding on the head. I clung onto the bars of the crush and gathered myself enough to realize both bullocks were standing patiently waiting for me to close the tail board which I duly did, only to realize I was losing blood.

Sometimes these "old men's Tablets" that thin your blood are not a good thing when ya geta ole in ya ed, anyone would think that there is greater pressure if the hole is at the bottom of the tank, but then this is a pumped leak, at the top of the "stack" but still it leaked at a worrying rate. Not wishing to stain the seats in the vehicle, I drew my jacket round to form a canopy on my lap whilst I drove the outfit down to the house where I sprinted (at my sprint) to the back door and got under the cold tap over the kitchen sink. A bit of firm pressure and after a few minutes it all but stooped bleeding (down to a drip). I threw my jacket shirt and jeans into a bucket of cold water to soak and put clean ones on again. Me wellingtons, well the last time I saw them in that state was when we used to kill and stick turkeys, caked with blood, wash them under the back yard tap.

In the meantime it felt safe enough for me to go through to the office to ring Mark, a chap who helps me on a part time basis, as and when needed. Well, now he was needed, he was not too far away, and he took the cattle down to market for me. Next I rang my daughter to come over, and she was able to take me to the notorious STAFFORD HOSPITAL,

(It's been in the national news over the last year and questions asked in parliament about the number of patient usually older patients, being lost through neglect, too busy looking at saving on their budget, not enough front line nurses).

Eileen my misses was the last to be told, as she can get very worried, it always looks so much worse when there is so much blood, (too much stress at her age is not good for her) she examined the wound and said get off and get it stitched.

By now it was 9am with about three people waiting in A&E (accident and emergency), we waited an hour only to be told they had no doctors on duty, and until one arrived, they could not proceed with any treatment. Another half hour and I was called through into the treatment cubicle where I could see a senior member of staff instructing a couple of young doctors of their routine, then eventually a full qualified doctor (at least I hope he was) came in with one of the new recruits, and went in details of what other pain or ailments other than what he could see, the proceeded to put in six stitches.

He made a neat job, and a plaster was stuck over the wound. It was not until the following day when the black eye began to appear. The result could be seen in the picture taken two days later.

How does the old saying go
A stitch in time save nine -- *in this case it could mean nine pints blood*

Chapter 30

Computers Read the Lot

Were in a plastic (card) revolution right now, and no doubt it will not be long before they get rid of the cheque book.

My first card a few years ago, I say a few years ago because I was well out of date with these sort of ideas, was copied, or cloned or the number stolen. The first I knew about it was when my statement came and it stated that I had bought a new television at a London store for £355. Of course the card was stopped albeit late, and fortunately no other things had been purchased from the card. A new card was sent the old one destroyed and the money lost was reinstated back into my account.

On looking back on what had happened or how the number had been stolen, each Friday we nip off to the super market to do the weekly shop, and that weekend I filled up with fuel and drew some cash from the cash point in Tesco's shop wall, and unbeknown to me and a lot of other people there was a scanner stuck over the hole where the card goes in and the numbers logged, quite a few other folk had been caught in the same scam that same day.

About a year previous to my financial experience, she indoors had her purse stolen in the same super market while pushing her trolley round the store. A youth had been watching her and at an opportune moment, rushed by and lifted the purse from a shoulder bag, I know it should not have been open, but these things happen.
Suppose you would call it a mugging. The alarm was soon raised, as a shelf stacker saw the incident and raced after the robber who legged it out of the store and

alongside the river Sow and over a foot bridge. On his way he must have stripped out the contents and threw the empty purse into the river. We went through the rigmarole of stopping the card and obtaining a replacement. Then over six months later we had a phone call from a Seven Trent river workman, his gang were working on weeding out the river Sow through the town, he had dragged out the stolen purse, looked, and the plastic card was still in it, he found our phone number from our name on the card, and the stolen purse was returned useless muddy and going rotten.

Another silly incident was when my card date expired and a new one sent in the post, on reading through the bumf that comes with the new card it said in no uncertain terms that the old one must be destroyed immediately. With that I grabbed the card and popped it through the shredder, only to realize I had shredded the new card. Needless to say I had an embarrassing call to the bank to explain what had happened and to plead to them to send yet another new card.

Suppose you could have called it a "senior moment".

Plastic Card

Down to do the shopping, they're open till very late
Paid for on a plastic card, flexible friend a mate,
A number that they call a pin, must be punched in right,
This can use any time, even day or night,
Slong as money's in the bank, it will spit it out,
Over drawn is evil, of money you've got a drought.
Spending more n what you' got, do ya sums all wrong,
The trouble that it causes, bank letters they are long,
Makes ya sweat and worry, and cannot settle down,
Pace about and have a shout, it gives ya face a frown.

Numbers Galore

Phone numbers and the mobile,
bank sort codes n' accounts,
Credit card that can be skimmed,
all ya savings trounce,
Car numbers and engine numbers
and chassis numbers too,
Model numbers part numbers,
colour codes pursue.

House numbers street numbers,
area post codes an all,
All across the country,
codes for counties large and small,
Field numbers, map numbers,
parish number long,
Acres turned to hectares,
if ya know where they belong.

SBI and there's IACS,
vendor as well,
PI and a Trader numbers,
and Stewardship numbers tell,
There's numbers for every thing,
for this that and tuther,
Fill ya head with confusion,
so many thing that got to cover.

Gallons turned to litres,
pounds and ounces gone to grams,
Miles turned to kilometres,
and foot to millimetre crammed

Therms have turned to Mj's,
power in Hp turned to Watts,
Heat is Btu to lbs,
is now into Joules per Kilogram it jots.

The moneys gone to Euros,
bank rate measures that,
Information all in plastic,
and its in your wallet sat,
Converted into bar codes,
so computers read the lot,
Nothing ever private now,
they know all of what you've got.

Money is like a sixth sense without which you cannot make a complete use of the other five.
W. Somerset Maugham (1874 - 1965

Chapter 31

We have a Cow and she's Real Mad

But only when we are trying to round them up, all the rest of the time out grazing with the other cows she is quite normal. If there is more than one person in the field she becomes aware she starts to get alerted, and if by chance we start to drive the herd towards the gate, her head goes up and ears pricked forward, and as the whole herd approach the exit of the field with her in the middle of the bunch, suddenly she charges out of the group in the opposite direction dodging any attempts' for us to stop her. It's a habit she has got into and we cannot even begin to try to calm her down, or break her of this syndrome. The last time we actually got her into the coral with the other cows was when we rounded them up to worm the calves. On that occasion we let the herd into a small field at the end of the lane, and left them in for twenty four hours. By that time they were all hungry and ready to be moved.

To put you in the picture, the coral is at the farm end of the lane, a number of fields with gates open into the lane, and at the far end, the end gate opens into the corner of a small field making it handy to walk the cattle down to the coral. On this occasion with them being hungry for more grass, we opened the gate and the herd moved naturally toward that corner, including the wild one. As I said she takes no notice as long as we stay on the tractor, she thinks we are just counting them as I do every morning. They all gradually walked into the lane grazing and pulling at the grass down the hedge banks, she was the only one standing confused in the gateway, first looking down the lane then back across the field to us in the tractor. It's like being in a hide, and well back across the field we waited, then finally she made her mind up to run and catch up with the others. When we followed she had caught up and mingled and was successfully got into the coral.

The time is fast approaching when the claves need to be weaned and the whole lot gathered again, but what worries me most is when we have to have them all in for testing, and have got to get them all in on that particular day and again three days later to read the results. Another problem as well is she has lost both her ear tags, I know the number, but just the thought on clamping her in the head yolk in the crush, and inserting two ear tags, if they hold still you can often get them into the same hole in the ear, but most likely we will have to punch them in as well as we can, more pain and suffering.

Where DO we get her confidence back from?.

We do have a good leader of the herd, no it's not him he's Winston he came and had a look round the house and garden

The Cows Have Got a Leader

The cows have got a leader,
and she watches all the while,
She knows exactly what ya doing,
sometimes make you smile,
Only got to touch the gate latch,
and up will go her head,
And walk towards the gateway,
without a word being said.

Go to count them every morning,
and check that they're all okay,
They think they want a new field,
and walk off all that way,
Oblige them at your peril,
as they mob you round the gate,
The fencings got to be strong,
if you've got to make them wait.

If more than one walks in the field,
leader walks the other way,
Takes the whole lot with her,
she must know its testing day,
Got to walk round whole dam field,
head them to the gate,
Seems that they have forgotten,
and vet's is here by eight.

Leader walking off right way,
the others following her lead,
Off towards the gateway,
but they're gathering speed,

All stop short of going through,
and start to circle round,
A young one makes a break for freedom,
loose the lot confound.

A bucket with a bit of corn,
the leaders up for that,
Always first one at the trough,
and give her a little pat,
She follows where you walking,
out off out down the lane,
Other think they're missing out,
and follow once again.

So cherish your old leader,
she can save you a lot of time,
Show the young cows where to go,
while she's in her prime,
Miss her when she finally goes,
to meet her maker's bullet,
End up as tough old leather boot's,
n' fill a of pack of suet.

―――――――――

The task of a leader is to get his people (in this case cows) from where they are to where they have not been.
Henry Kissinger (1923-)

Chapter 32

The hay elevator

I Remember the old cast iron wheels

Long old elevator, use to pitch the corn,
High in the hay barn, before the combine born,
After harvest it was thatched, with straw all long,
Stood out all the winter, next harvest came along.

When it became redundant, thatch it rotted away,
Right through the timber, and start off decay,
Eventually a match was put, and burned the timber out
The iron was scrapped except, the wheels they're still about.

There is four of these wheels off the old elevator, two large and two a bit smaller.

As long back as I can remember loose hay was pitched onto the wagons with pitch forks by hand, and then from the wagon drawn by the shire horses to a hay barn or built into a hay stack in a convenient spot in the corner of the field. Then hay loaders came in they called them pitchers, and at the stack came elevators. When I took over this farm in 1985, at the end of the hay barn was what remained of an old elevator. The previous farmer's father had purchased it a good many years ago being one of the first in the area. At the end of hay and corn harvest all the inside storage was full, so it was folded away into its transport mode pulled round to the end of the barn and thatched. Batons (as opposed to bales) are straight straw after it has been threshed and put through a binder, tied with two bonds of string and around five foot long. These were laid length ways all the length of the elevator pyramid fashion, then further batons of straw were straightened and used to thatch the whole of the elevator. Being made of wood with cast iron wheel and cast brackets and pullies it had to be kept dry when not in use. However when pickup balers came in the elevator fell out of use it just stood and stood year after year with its old thatch rotting away, and as rain soaked through it rotted the timbers until it resembled a muck ruck with wheels.

    It came to me to clear up the old elevator in my first year here, and before next harvest started we stuffed more dry straw underneath and chuck a match in to burn it out. All the ironwork was sorted out of the ashes and chucked onto the scrap ruck save the wheels, the engine had been removed a long time ago and sold, and it had been a Bamford single cylinder water cooled petrol engine with an open flywheel and a flat pulley on the drive shaft.

The Scrap Ruck

I got a pile of scrap iron, and it builds up real fast,
And another round the corner, where I dropped it last,
I save it just in case, nothings ever chucked away,
Piles of it everywhere, It might come in one day.

Broken bits of tractor, and its off cut bits of steel,
Some is thick, some is thin, and some a bit of wheel,
Angle iron in six foot lengths, some point was a bed,
Other bits chucked into rucks, some still painted red.

Nettles growing through it, and it makes a nesting site,
For rats and mice n' vermin, who are only out at night,
Disturbed they run like mad, get away from you or me,
And where do they head for, scrap ruck home with glee.

I'm looking for a bit of metal, the size ta mend a gate,
Seen some in the scrap ruck, but I can't locate,
Know where I chucked it, don't know which pile it's in,
Turn each pile over and see, praps neath that pile of tin.

It's rusting in the winter, the snow and rain soaks in,
It's rusty and it's flaking, and its no use for welding,
Dunt know why I saved it, cus price of scraps sky high,
Have to have a clear out, home for rats and mice deny.

A harvest of peace is produced from a seed of contentment.
American Proverb

Chapter 33

Cattle out Wintering

It looks like the beginning of a two week cold snap; the cattle seem to have grown a longer woolly coat almost overnight, and it's still only third week in November. In general the stock has grown well through the summer and with a reasonable quality of silage to feed should be able to maintain condition on throughout the winter. As always we have a few that have lost an ear tag, in one case lost both, but then that's not unusual, most often it's alongside sheep netting that they get caught or round the ring feeder that the missing tags are found.

The gates are nearly all open between the fields and the herd is ranging across most of the farm, gleaning round the maize stubbles and hedge banks and wildlife strips. We have offered silage and just a few cows are coming back to the ring feeders and pecking at it. A few days on and we have a covering of snow and they are now on full silage winter feeding, although there is always some that prefer to top up on any grass they can nuzzle down to and pull at hedge banks.

Now I am a cow and telling me tale,

Now I am a cow and telling me tale,
Owd Fred he's writing it down,
Started life as a little seed,
with hundreds I'm not on me own,
Ventualy sent and injected,
into a poor old mother cow,
Met with an egg and we welded,
together held tight somehow.

Started to double in size,
and a head with eyes was formed,
Then four legs and a tail,
growing in a ball transformed,
Front legs started to point forward,
with me chin on me knees,
Too big to stay where I was,
getting shoved out if you please.

Front feet they're out in the cold,
me nose is feeling fresh air,
Then me eyes and head they are outside,
no going back in their,
Me shoulder and hips it's a struggle,
but suddenly drop in the straw,
I'm hear, I'm wet, and I'm breathing,
out here its cold and it's raw.

Mother she's got up and lickin,
all over me face and me belly,
I sit up and shaking me ed,
to get up on me legs they're like jelly,
Up on me back legs okay,
onto me knees I'm looking for a teat,
All round me mother's big belly,
om looking for something to eat.

Alright now that I've found it,
a bunt and the milk flows right quick,
Me belly its full and I'm drying out,
mother gives me a reassuring lick,
Off to hide and have a good rest,
and mother to find some food,
The gaffer Owd Fred he lifts me leg,
bull or heifer he's just being rude.

A couple of days he holds me down,
in me ear puts a big tag,
Does the same again in the other,
balance me ed so it doesn't sag,
Some reason he looks under me tail,
rubber ring he's no need to use,
Writes my number into his little book,
he's old but he's no right to abuse.

The gaffer Owd Fred he opened the gate,
out onto grass to play,
After a week I found I can run,
and found some others who say,
Get ya ed down and taste the grass,
big field all bright and green,
All the adults do nothing else,
to fill their belly they're keen.

At three months I've got a cough,
all me mates the same,
And me tail its getting dirty,
only one thing we can blame,
It's worms that got into me belly,
and they're hanging onto me gut,
Taking goodness out of me food,
belly thinks me throats been cut.

The gaffer goes and gets the stuff,
and pours it along our backs,
It soaks right into me spine,
soaks right in and me belly reacts,
Loosens all the teeth,
of worms and lice and all,
They fall out behind me,
new pasture now is the call.

Good summer out on the grass,
and autumn chill is in the air,
He's got us gathered in the pen,
what he's doing I'm not aware,
All the mothers he's letting out,
and now backed up a trailer,
End of the race he's pushing us in,
he's nothing more than a jailer.

Big load of us all frightened and hot,
unloaded into a pen,
Walking around trying to get out,
shouting agen and agen,
Me voice getting soar after three days,
milk I want to suck,
But this is the end I'm eating hay,
mother's left us all in the muck.

So here I am, inside with my mates,
were being fed every day,
All bedded up and comfortable,
having silage as well as hay,
A lick of corn and a mineral block,
clean water out of the mains,
It beats the water out of the brook,
it only comes out of farm drains

.Its testing time, we run down the race,
vet lifts up me tail,
Shoves it right up almost over me back,
then he sticks in a nail,
No it wasn't it's a needle,
a bottle is on the end,
Full to the top with my blood,
I hope the hole will mend.

Now it looks like spring time,
and the grass is growing again,
Nice to have a good run round,
for that I won't complain,
Grass it's so nice and sweet, a
fter all that dry old hay,
I'm bigger now and twelve months old,
too big now to play.

Over in a distant field,
I can see my mother again,
Not allowed to go and see her,
she's really looks well and then,
To my dismay she's got a new calf,
a brother or sister for me,
Bunting round and drinking MY milk,
how terribly cruel it can be.

I've lost me rough coat from winter,
and new short hair has grown,
In the sunshine it shows off real well,
glossy with lick marks alone,
I spend the whole summer in deep grass,
and lie in the shade of a tree,
Were growing now and nearly adult,
my mother won't recognise me.

All my group were two years old,
and a new young bull turned in,
It's a Hereford with a big white face,
he's running us round in a spin,
I'm not able to tell you what happens next,
but catches us one at a time,
One or two of us every day,
just getting to know us all in our prime.

Second winter its out at grass,
and not a blade to be seen,
Silage in a ring feeder,
as much as we want nice and clean,
Frost and snow, and cold winds
from the north, shelter under the wood,
Long woolly coat on me back,
tails to the wind is the way we all stood.

Me belly its getting real big,
and it's not that I've eaten a lot,
And getting swollen between me legs,
soar and hard and hot,
Then I got a real bad pain,
so off on me own to lay down,
A push and a push and a push again,
me water bag its blown.

A real big strain and it stretches me bum,
a lump I'm pushing out
A couple more and it drops right out,
the relief as I give a shout,
Pick me ed up and av a look round,
me very own calf just their,
Jump to me feet and give it a lick,
all wet and wobbly and sticky the hair.

I'm now a mother and lickin,
all over his face and his belly,
He's sit up and shaking is ed,
to get up on his legs they're like jelly,
Up on his back legs okay,
onto his knees and looking fa a teat,
All round my big belly,
he's looking for something to eat.

Alright now that he's found it,
a bunt and the milk flows right quick,
His belly it's full and he's drying out,
so I give him a reassuring lick,
Off to hide and have a good rest,
I go to find some food,
The gaffer Owd Fred he lifts his leg,
bull or heifer he's just being rude.

A couple of days he holds him down,
in his ear puts a big tag,
Does the same again in the other,
balance his ed so it doesn't sag,
Some reason he looks under his tail,
rubber ring he's got to use,
Writes my number into his little book,
he's old but he's no right to abuse.

So it is that life goes on,
and had ten calves one every year,
Got used to what the routine is,
now I'm the leader it's clear,
Show the others where to go,
and how to dodge a test,
And wait by the gate for a new field;
shoot past Owd Fred do our best.

He gave me a name and it's Chocky,
stuck with me right from a calf,
Got to know how Owd Fred ticks,
meck im chases round not by half,
Now he's got a real mean trick,
tasty feed in bottom of his bucket,
Can't resist I've got to follow,
into the corral then we get to suck it.

I've reared a lot of good calves,
for Owd Fred to fatten for beef,
Om getting tired and old,
to retire it would be a relief,
But no he's keeping me on,
to calve again in the shed,
And him to tell his farming tales,

―――――――

Sacred cows make the best hamburgers.
Mark Twain (1835-1910)

Church Farm when it was a working Farm

Capter 34

The Persistent Escapee (cow)

A cow that persistently gets out, gets better at it, she learns to jump or hop over slack wire, learns to push rails down and push at the legs of electric fence posts, and push through weak places in hedges. Bulls soon learn to lift gates off there hinges or as a neighbour's bull has done he will break wooden gates in two. It's a matter of not letting them get into the habit of getting out, "the grass is always greener etc". A secure fence, with barbed wire pulled up tight, barbed wire put up slack looking like a washing line is no good.

Cattle are a herd animal and they will all follow a leader, and if it's the leader that is that persistent one that is always getting out you're in trouble. They all have their own personality and it shows when studied, particularly when gathered and handled. They range from the one that steps forward to have its shoulder scratched to the one that will charge at you when cornered, and as for the newly calved cow even the most placid cow can turn nasty and charge. Their behavior often follows in families, and how the mother behaves is passed down to the calf at a very young age, almost a perception or body language is read by the calf from birth, and if it's the bull that has a bad attitude being handled or driven, he too will influence the attitude of the herd.

There is often the one with the wicked eye, and the one that lifts her head up and pricks her ears at the first sign of strange movement in the field. Some will venture forward and investigate to see what's going on, the others follow by herd nature, and some will disappear away behind the herd or into a hollow where they cannot be seen. It only takes one cow to give out a Bellow rather than a Moo, and the whole herd will go running to investigate what's going on. It sometimes happens when assisting a calving, when the cow gives one last big push and a bellow at the same time, then is a good time to retreat rapidly.

Back to the one that gets out, I solved the problem by selling her, she would get out into the farm track and graze down the hedge banks, then instead of getting back the way she had come, she would walk down to a small group of ten houses at the end of the track, walk into the gardens and round to the back (all open plan, silly idea) and hop over their back fence into her field.

When this had gone on for quite a few months the folk in the houses were getting very angry, every foot print sank deep into the lawns, the evidence was there, the row of peas were being grazed and dung pats left in exchange. The gardens are a foot or so above field level and while the fence was a sensible height from the field, from the gardens it was only knee height to the cow. Some of the gardens had wooden panel fences with my barbed wire fence on the field side others are fancy post and rail or chain link wire mesh, all were pitched at a height that the occupants could see out across the fields. At this point I must say it nearly always happened during the night, and when they rang me to complain and I went to investigate only the foot prints were there.

I finished up putting a new gate on the end of the lane; the cow then walked through the lane side hedge into the first house garden a six foot tall beech hedge and continued with the same route back to the field. Fortunately she was the only one doing it, and she was so persistent that the only option was to sell her. She was a young well-built cow only had three calves and I thought it would be a good idea if she gave someone else a bit of "entertainment", NIMBY (not in my backyard)

The cows are Charolais Angus Simmental crosses put to a Hereford bull, calves are April born

In the mid 1950's vets were recommending worming young stock with a new product called phenothiazine. This was a green powder and had to be mixed with water and a pint or so was pour down their throats. (drenched)

I Remember Father's Cattle

I remember father counting,
cattle each and every day,
He counts and looks at every one,
to see they're all OK,
Now one day he see's one cough,
and then it was another.
If we don't do something quickly,
we'll be in a bit of bother.

So off down he goes to get,
some wormer in a rush,
And back he comes and reads the label,
says get them in a crush,
No crush have we, but four strong lads,
we'll get them in a stable,
Mix water and green powder in a bucket,
put it on the table.

Four long neck bottles we did find,
for dosing all the cattle,
Phenothiozine, it's called,
and keep it stirred or it will settle,
The pop had gone as we made sure;
we loved the fizzy taste,
One pint and half was dose that's needed,
over dose was waste.

Pint ladle and a funnel now,
into the bottled it was measured,
Us lads went in among the stock,
as tight a they could be,
The bottles we did pass to one,
who had ones chin held high,
Uptip the med-sin to back of throat,
do not look down or ni.

The cow that coughs, coughs both ends,
and chuck it back they try,
Its just a waste as we were told,
ut hits you in the eye,
Soon learn to leave it quickly,
as soon as we could shift,
As dosing cattle get there own back,
now who's being thrift.

We often wondered why we lads,
had grown so big and strong,
When other lads around us,
were only lean and long,
Put it down to fresh air,
and read farmers weekly magazine,
But all the time it wasn't, twas Phenothiazine.

―――――――――

Many of us have heard (herd) opportunity knocking at our door (garden), but by the time we unhooked the chain, pushed back the bolt, turned two locks, and shut off the burglar alarm, it was gone (the cow).
Author unknown

Chapter 35

Story of Hobble End Cottages

In one of our farthest fields, situated about a mile east of the village was a pair of cottages known as Hobble End. There was no road not even a cart track to them, only a foot path, one of which led directly to the village then the other way it was about two miles into town. They were estate cottages, one occupied by a woodman and the other a farm worker. They were heated and the cooking done on open fires and lit with oil lamps and candles. All that remains now is the rich black soil of the garden, and a few bricks that keep coming up every time it is ploughed. In the hedgerow is the remains of the old front wicket and a galvanized pipe that once carried water from the well to the houses. There is no chance of buried treasure as it was very poor families that lived there, every now and then bits of metal do get ploughed up, it's very often old hand tools used in the garden and bits of broken pottery. Down in the small brook that ran by in the hollow was another wicket where the footpath crosses onto the neighbouring farm. When any family flitted in or out, it was with horse and cart, and the same when they wanted coal or logs. At the fare end of the garden was the inevitable toilet that needed emptying as soon as the bucket was full. It was the practice to dig a deep hole and keep pouring it in, then soil it over, no wonder the soil was so dark and rich in these old gardens. In local terms this type of toilet was called "bucket and chuckit". Needless to say these latrines were dug well away from the 'well'.

They also had a pig sty where a pig would be fattened on scraps and waste from the house and garden, and eventually killed and cured for feeding their large families.

How we Lived in our Old House

Insulations none existent,
big jumper you must ware,
Half timbered single brick,
few inches plaster of horse hair,
Frosty weather glistens inside,
a fridge you could compare,
Roof half filled with starling's nests,
built up over the years.

Kitchens the warmest place,
coal fire in big old range,
Heats the oven and boils,
the kettle on the chimney crane,
Boils the taters and stew,
toast the bread on a fork,
From the ceiling hangs a cloths drier,
lifts and lowers on cord.

Bedroom bove the kitchen,
only room upstairs warm,
Usually the kids have this room, t
hat is always the norm,
Other rooms are chilled and cold,
cool in summer though,
This is how we lived them days,
kids now will never know.

Old iron bedstead webbed with steel,
straw mattress on the top,
Then feather mattress covered
with a white sheet she'd pop,

Mother made a groove up this,
dropped us into bed,
A sheet two blankets and eiderdown,
feather pillow lay ya head.

Best front room not often used,
too posh to use every day,
Used over Christmas and party's,
best crockery out on display,
Fathers roll top desk in there,
his bills and letters wait to pay,
Always locked cus of cash in their,
he always had last say.

Now heating was a big open fire,
ingle nook chimney above,
Logs as long as ya can lift,
one end on the fire to shove,
The bigger the fire, bigger
the draught across the floor,
The heat goes up the chimney,
fresh air comes in under the door.

A cellar beneath front room,
brick steps leading down,
Couple of vents to the garden,
the mesh with weeds overgrown,
Air circulation its not good,
and musty damp and wet,
Timber in the floor above,
gone weak and springy pose a threat.

Old iron bedstead webbed with steel,
straw mattress on the top,
Then feather mattress covered
with a white sheet she'd pop,

Mother made a groove up this,
dropped us into bed,
A sheet two blankets and eiderdown,
feather pillow lay ya head.

Best front room not often used,
too posh to use every day,
Used over Christmas and party's,
best crockery out on display,
Fathers roll top desk in there,
his bills and letters wait to pay,
Always locked cus of cash in their,
he always had last say.

Now heating was a big open fire,
ingle nook chimney above,
Logs as long as ya can lift,
one end on the fire to shove,
The bigger the fire, bigger
the draught across the floor,
The heat goes up the chimney,
fresh air comes in under the door.

A cellar beneath front room,
brick steps leading down,
Couple of vents to the garden,
the mesh with weeds overgrown,
Air circulation its not good,
and musty damp and wet,
Timber in the floor above,
gone weak and springy pose a threat.

A room with settlass all way round,
there to salt the pig,
Not been used now for many a year,
doesn't look so big,

Salt has drawn up the brickwork,
all through to outside
Bricks are flaking and rotting,
replace section of bricks decide.

Mother kept a big tin bath,
hung on a nail outside back door,
Brought it in to the hearth,
filled with kettle and big jug she pour,
Youngest first then nother kettle,
warm it agen for the second,
Cold night our steaming little bodies,
hot crisp towel it beckoned.

So we kids lived in the big kitchen,
our bedroom top of back stairs,
Long old sofa under the window,
father had his own armchair,
Big old peg rug in front of the fire,
we played and sat on that,
Large old radio in the window,
then hurray first tele in front we sat.

———————

Every mile is two in winter.
George Herbert (1593 - 1633)

Chapter 36

Low Cost Production, Milk Marketing Board 1962

So all in all you reap what you sow, you cannot keep robbing the producer, in this case the cow.

It started when I joined a Milk Marketing Board scheme called 'Low Cost Production'. November 1962. Much to my disgust I seemed to always be in the lower quarter of the chart / league table.
You take up on all the latest ideas, when ya young and think you can improve even on them. But as time and experience will learn you, let someone else try them out (new ideas), and if they are still good ideas a few years later that's the time to take them up. Some expensive mistakes have been made over the years, when caution would have been the prudent thing to do.

Over stocking is one of them, it started when I joined a Milk Marketing Board scheme called 'Low Cost Production'. The coordinator called every month to update all the figures and the different margins, from cost per gallon over bought in feed, production from home grown feeds, and labour costs. These were all logged into a chart with about twenty two other participating farms with the best performing ones at the top and those with lowest margins at the bottom. Of course each farm/farmer was incognito and you could only identify your own farm by a code number issued by the coordinator. Much to my disgust I seemed to always be in the lower quarter of the chart, and so there was great incentive to get nearer to the top. More fertilizer was bought, the cows were strip grazed rigidly with a back fence the nitrogen was applied for the re-growth, and a little later in the scheme we were encouraged to lay it all out in twenty one paddocks, one paddock a day and again fertilized after grazing. This all went on for just over four years, the cows numbers increased, stock feed potatoes and carrots were fed to supplement the winter feed, and we mixed our own dairy corn from a recommended ration compounded up from straights and costed out.

It was made up of

Home grown rolled barley	
Sugar beet pulp	
Flaked maize	
Sweetened palm kernel	
Bran	
Soya bean meal	
Fish meal	
Groundnut flakes	
And Minerals	

    The barley was put through the roller and it dropped directly onto the barn floor, the other ingredient were weighed up in the loft and tipped through a convenient hole in the floor. The pile was then mixed by hand with a huge shovel turning it three times
    The cost worked out at £19- 7s- 6d per ton as against a propriety dairy cake of between £60 & £70 pound a ton. All calculations were done literally by hand, it was before calculators came out and the coordinator added subtracted, divided, and multiplied everything on a slide rule.

Low Cost Production, Milk Marketing Board 1962

[Milk Marketing Board Low Cost Production form, one day check on production costs, dated 7/11/1962]

The chart above is the original or should I say the initial one filled in by Mr. Woodriffe our coordinator/ adviser, and it was November 1962 over fifty years ago.

I may be wrong but going on the figures above my mixture comes out at just below £20 a ton and the Diary Cake at the top come out at over £60 a ton, not quite right me thinks. If any keen costing students or older 'pharts' like me can get it any different please let me know. I have all the
Invoices for the soya, fishmeal, groundnut etc. so I could check that for prices

There is an average line at the bottom that would not scan, and lined up should read
13.4 / 9.94 / 6.98 / 0.64 / 17.56 / 5.46 / 64 / 49 / 2.12 / 3.03 / 9.07 / 0.61

This is the matching resultant chart that we got back at the end of the month that is my line third line from the bottom of the table, **code /159**. Margin per gallon 9.85, and 39 in herd, 35 in milk.

This was the only time I managed to top my group April 1964 see **code /159**. We had turned the cows out onto some early grass; all the cows were in milk. It was only through the summer months that I could compete on the league table. Eventually I found out that some of the top ones in the winter had larger acreages of stubbles and sugar beet fields to range over and young stock away on another area of land, giving them an unfair advantage over me stuck tightly on 96 acres with quite a few young stock and follower.

By the report from the MMB and the farming press it was a great success, for me we raised our output and margins, but ended up with a whole herd of very thin cows, some almost skeletons. Another aspect was to calve the heifers down at two years old, some of which had not attained the required growth to reach a reasonable lactation.

The calving index was another thing that was important in these calculations, ours was around 370 day calving when we started, and as the cows got into a lower and lower state so this rose to around the 400day mark.

So all in all you reap what you sow, you cannot keep robbing the producer, in this case the cow, and occasionally in life its better to back off a little, work under a bit less pressure, the cows and yourself are a lot fitter.

You may not have made your fortune, there is always someone in life who does thing better than you (or claim to), and that has never changed all my life.

The Cow Chain

At one time cows were all tied up,
in stalls to milk and feed,
Each one knew its own place,
not much room indeed,
When young they didn't like it,
but soon learned where to go,
Twice every day it was for them,
walking to and fro.

Out to daytime pastures,
to distant fields to graze,
Back again for milking
on long fine summer days,
Walk into their own shed,
and finding their own stall,
Standing there to be chained,
got to chain them all.

Each stall holds a pair of cows,
left and right they learn,
Once they know their own side,
one word n' they discern,

"Come over" spoken to them,
they know you're coming through,
The pair will part, n' chain them up,
n' stand their cud to chew.

A scoop of corn while milking,
then wait till milked the lot,
Loosed off the chains they wander,
out to pasture we allot,
Clean the sheds and clean the stalls,
till milking comes again,
For to tie them up you always need,
good strong shiny chain.

———-

Knowledge is the only instrument of production that is not subject to diminishing returns.
John Maurice Clarke. *Economist*

Chapter 37

The June Returns 1961

My first year farming in my own right 1961

Just dug out an old diary from just fifty years ago, and on looking at the page where I recorded the June Returns 1961, (a statutory form sent out by the Ministry every June) it started with Crops.

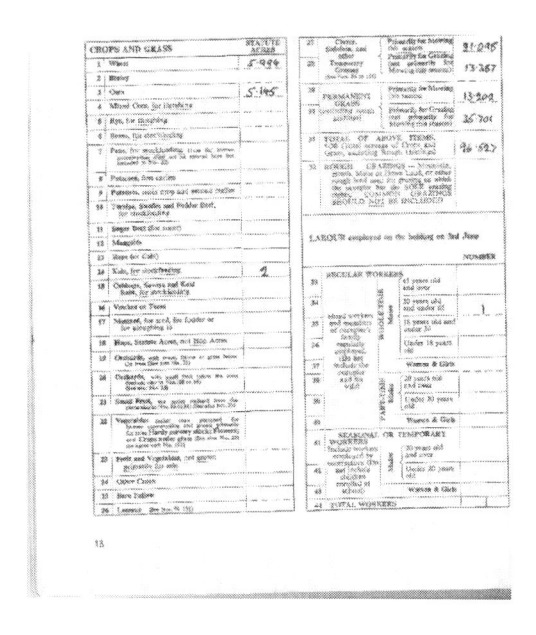

Crops above. Then onto livestock below

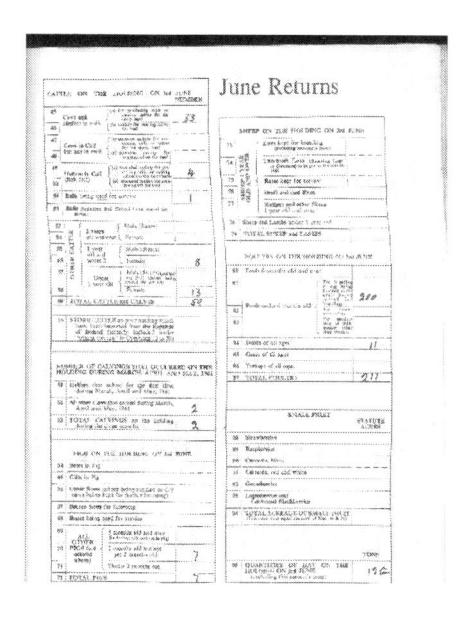

Then to the grass land and any other spurious crops that might be grown around the country

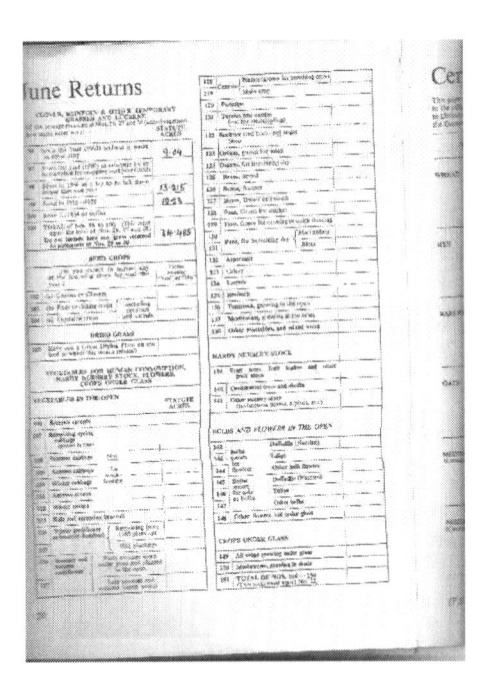

Total area was 96 acres, which was a popular acreage on the estate as four or even five farms were 96 acres or very close to it, with three others into the 120 to 140 acre bracket.

Looking back I had almost six acres of wheat and five acres of oats, and looking further down the year it was bindered and stooked in the fields. Later still in the diary, into the winter we had the contractor came with his threshing set and stationary baler, combines were only just getting about, and it was a contractor that had the only one in our area. Only two year before in 1959 when I was at farm college, we were taught how to pull and top sugar beet by hand, (a job we had been doing for three years at home) the students and the college farm workmen had cleared the beet off the headlands then a sugar beet harvester was brought in, the first one I had seen and only one in our part of the world, on trial, and as a demonstrator.

Back to the 'returns', two acres of marrow stem kale was drilled and singled by hand hoe, and some new sown grass seeds, and short term leys, finishing up with the balance of acreage as permanent pasture. On to the labour section, one twenty year old man who took home his first wage packet from me £7-10s-6d , or if you bring it up to new money values, £7-52 and a half p. for a whole weeks work.

The cattle amounted to thirty three cows, four in calf heifers, one Friesian bull, eight yearlings, and thirteen heifer calves. That was the limit of stalls we had at that time as the cows would be tied by the neck with a chain to each stall. It was around this time that a new concept of housing cows other than stalls and deep bedding had just been invented, the cow cubicle. The dimensions were critical and great publicity was given to the idea in the farming press, I built a small row of cubicle stalls free standing with its own roof as a lean-to alongside the cow shed. They proved very successful and some ten years later purchased and put up a sixty four stall cubicle house that we erected ourselves; every other stall extended up to support the roof.

Pigs, we had seven store pigs for fattening, no sheep, and two hundred laying hens kept in a deep litter poultry pen, and eleven geese that ran out to the stream that runs close by in the fields behind the farm.

Another section in the front of the diary was the amount of milk sold that year This showed we were mainly spring calving, peaking in April when the cows went out to grass. The bottom line added up and divided by 33 cows make an average of 830 gallons per cow, the aim in them days of recorded herds were a thousand gallons per cow.

This was a first year, perhaps a greater number of first calf heifers, and a certain amount was used to suckle the thirteen calves reared to at least two months of age. I shall have to look back at the national milk records to see when I started recording, as that shows what each cow produces, not how much is sold.

On the chart above it seems April the 20th was the peak of the milk per day sold in that year 1961

Chapter 38   Rats

They are a never ending problem, but not as bad as they used to be back sixty or more years ago. They would come down from the fields as the autumn got colder and into the stacks and bays filled with shoffs of wheat and oats, the stacks outside were thatched and for moisture would work their way up onto the top of the rick and make holes in the new thatching.

It was often ringed with small mesh wire netting while the threshing machine was working on it so as to make sure we caught as many as we could, a lot jumped from the top as the thatch was being removed, all us kids would be armed with nut stick with a knob on the end, and great excitement as they run and dodged about.

A good dog, my dog caught most but he almost came unstuck when he picked up a rat just as a big knobbed stick came down heavy and hit him on his head and knocked him out as he killed the rat. He came round after a short while and was back at work after a few days.

The sacks of wheat had to be stacked two high in rows apart so the cats could get between them, failure to do this, within a few days, while waiting transport rats would nibble hole always seemed to be in the bottom of the sack. When they are loaded, sacks with holes would be under weight, and would have to be re-bagged and re-weighed, a lot of time spent for not stacking the sacks open in rows.

Just occasionally, a rat has come into the house, and the one I relate back to happed midafternoon, and while we were having a break from work having a cup of tea.

While we were all sitting talking a rat crept round the corner of the house and ran in through the open back door, one of our group saw in the corner of his eye, what he thought was a rabbit. Mid roars of laughter it took him a while to convince the rest of us of what he claimed to see. Once we had taken him seriously we put our cups down and proceeded to search the house and the rooms that it could have hopped into.

It was in a down stairs bedroom that we eventually detected some movement, as it scuttled under a bed, the under other furniture, when it ran across the room and under a wardrobe we saw for ourselves that it was in fact a large rat. Right we thought we had got it cornered, all exits from the wardrobe were covered, and then one of us got down on hands and knees with a walking stick to flush it out. But to our surprise a rat could not be seen, it seemed a mystery where it had disappeared to, as we had guarded the wardrobe from when we saw it run under there. It had not got inside the wardrobe, unless it had suddenly made a rat hole into it while we waited, then realized it had clawed its way up between the wall and the back of the furniture. On assessing what height and roughly where it was, the door was opened the cloths parted and a large size eleven boot stamped heavily on the spot where it was thought to be. The rat slide down the wall to the floor crushed and dead, we moved the wardrobe forward, only to see a long slick of blood all down the wall and on the back of the wardrobe which had to be cleaned up quickly before it stained and dried. If it had not been seen at that moment, we could have been living with it for weeks, plenty of places for it to dig in for a long stay, under floor boards in the cellar, and in the loft roof space.

A rat is a rat is a rat for the cat,
The dogs got my dinner n' he's getting fat,

When the water reaches the upper level, follow the rats.
Claude Swanson (1862-1939

Chapter 39

First Land Rover a "Rag Top" Diesel

I bought my first land rover second hand some fifty years ago, it was a green diesel rag top, the one with a full canvas top forward over the driver, "Rag Top". We always drove about in it with the back flap rolled up leaving two tensioning straps down to each side of the drop tail gate.

It was difficult to start in winter and when it did start it pothered and puffed light blue smoke everywhere it went. When starting the engine in a car park particularly if it was a multi-story car park, you had to make sure there was no one walking by, the engine was started only when you were ready to go and when you knew you could drive straight out and onto the road. When driving along it was not so noticeable, smoke was diluted so to speak and the engine warmed up.

I was told by a mechanic who knew about such things that if I slackened the bolts holding the injector pump, and put a large pair of stilsons (big spanner) to grip the pump and turn it slightly while the engine was running, to adjust the timing it should solve the smoke problem.

Well it did to some extent but we were ready to change it for a new petrol version, rag top short wheel base dark green model.

Out on the road with the family "in the back" we got stuck in traffic, it was stop start, stop start, and the car following was teasing our kids who were sitting along mud wing shoulders each side in the back with two almost leaning out the back with just the tension straps of the canvas for support. Each time the traffic stopped the following car rolled close up to the back of us, worrying the kids and making them squeal thinking there was going to be an accident just stopping inches from our drawbar. After half a dozen stops we were on a downhill gradient and it was a matter of just letting the Land Rover just coast forward then stop, and the following car was doing the same and still stopping just inches from us.

As you may or may not be aware, those old Land Rovers had a red knob to pull to stop the engine that meant that when the ignition switch was switched off the engine kept running. It also meant that with the ignitions switched off the stop lights do NOT work, so on the next pull forwards, we came to a stop with the ignition off , no brake lights, the following car not giving his full attention that we had already stopped rolled smartly into our drawbar knob splitting his number plate and denting his ego. Needless to say on the next stop our brake lights worked perfectly and he kept a respectable distance. It was a day our kids will remember for a long while, but of course with today's road regulations they would not be allowed to "ride in the back" and with no seat belts.

The second Land Rover was a petrol one also with a "Rag top". This new one was a treat to drive and used for everything from going on holiday, to looking cattle down on the meadows and taking cattle to market and kids to school. The big problem on looking back was the ford that had to be forded sometimes only six inches deep more often a foot deep, and in flood up to three feet deep. At that depth we used only went through with the tractor.

After a few years the gritty water in the brakes soon wore out the brake pads and of course rusted the brake pipes and with the new MOT testing brake pipes had to be replaced, a few years on and the brake hubs that the brake pads rub on had worn badly. When new brake linings were fitted, half the adjustment was taken up just to get the linings to touch the hub. Ten years down the line the back cross member had to be replaced and welded in, the bolts holding the drawbar for the trailer had pulled through the one wall of the cross member, arrived home from market one day with the drawbar knob swinging about on two bolt that had pulled through six inches and hanging low.

Not long after that problem was solved a spring shackle on the rear of the front spring had broken and rusted loose, with another big hole in the chassis, that was patched and the bolt made secure again. Next was the body on the driver's side was listing and decidedly low, it was the cross member under the driver's seat that had broken away, this again was sorted out and a new one welded in place, it must have been difficult to find solid metal to weld to. But when the old member was removed, it held one end of the fuel tank and the end of the fuel tank fell out, so a new fuel tank was fitted. The alloy body work was good, the engine too, and it looked quite smart for a working Land Rover but you could push a screwdriver through the sides of the main chassis, such was the rot and rust, so it had to be got rid of or sold.

Why do they advertise and sell them as rot proof when only the alloy panels of the body are rot proof, but then we were on the extreme of testing it with driving through the ford any number of times a day for all the years I owned it. The rest of its demise and its sale is told in the poem below.

I Remember My Old Land Rover

I had a Land Rover it was very useful,
it was my only car,
Went everywhere in it,
and towed both the trailers off a far,
The weekly shopin piled in the back,
canvas flap pulled down,
Also took the girls to school,
sometimes to a party in a gown,

I went down fields counting cattle
and through the ford every day,
Always it got wet from the brook,
started rotting the chassis away,
One day it started to list,
and run down low on one side,
Thought it was a puncture but no,
cross member to body subside.

Took it to be repaired
and have a new cross member fitted,
Being close to end of fuel tank,
that too with rot submitted,
Ventualy we got it back,
though it was only away three days,
Vowed never to go through the ford again,
that was only a faze.

On the passenger side in the foot well,
a plate of steel was rotting,
Mud from the road splashing through,
enough soil in there for potting,
On a dry day the girls they watched the road,
till we hit a puddle,
Their feet were not quite big enough,
to cover hole and the rattle

A square of plywood placed over the hole,
so they could not see out,
In rough weather it blew it off,
revealed a bigger hole worn-out,
Some holes were beginning to show,
along the chassis rails,
Think its time to move it on,
put in the local rag under motor sales.

Thinking it was almost scrap,
didn't hold out too much hope,
Who would buy a thing like this;
he must be a silly dope,
Only had one reply to this,
a young man and his girlfriend came,
Parked the Land Rover long side a wall,
only saw good part of the frame.

A friend of mine he parked on the road,
and he stood back a little,
They thought it was another buyer,
they didn't bother to haggle,
Pulled out his money all in fivers,
and paid me on the spot,
Should have charged a lot more money,
but happy with what I've got.

I asked them what they had in mind,
for this old wreck of mine,
They're going on holiday to Norway,
to see the fiords and alpine,
Its engine was in tip top order,
and the gearbox that's OK,
Its just the bit that hold all together,
that I forgot to say.

In retrospect I could advise,
when they finished their break,
It would last for two weeks,
then push into fiord from highest peak,
Never heard from them again, s
o don't know if they survived,
Or what happened to my old Rover,
think it must have died.

Quote. **It is better to wear out than rust out**
Bishop Richard Cumberland

Chapter 40

Farm Dispersal Sales

At one time there used to be quite a few dispersal sales on the run up to March 25th when tenancies would be timed to change or end in retirement. Now there is only the odd one locally attracting a lot of interest from a wide area, these are timed to take place on a Saturdays when the maximum number of folk are able to attend.

They are a social occasions with not everyone going just to purchase, more often it's an opportunity to have a look round the farm and building that otherwise you would not be able to do, (it's called being nosy), everyone in a cheerful and generally happy mood. The prices attained at these sales are generally very good for the seller and sometimes neighbouring farms are allowed to enter their surplus items which bulk up the sale attracting even more folk.

It's a lot of work in the run up to sale date, items being dragged out of the back of sheds and buildings that have not seen the light of day in a good many years, it is these sort of things that attract collectors and enthusiasts of every kind. During the sale when bidding gets brisk, there is banter as well as bidding with the price going beyond what the item was originally valued at, two bidders hanging on trying to outbid each other it all to the good of the outgoing farmer, and make for a cheerful and happy atmosphere.

Part used and pre-warn or worn out right down to scrap iron, everything goes, the rusty seized up, the rotten with woodworm, the bent and twisted, everything has to go

The Farm Sale

The years have come the years have gone,
its time to sell the lot,
And now I've got to organize,
the sale of all I've got,
To pull it out the sheds and then,
n' lay it out in rows,
For all and everyone who comes, t
o have a dam good nose.

The tools and all machinery,
bought it years ago,
Ploughed the land and worked it,
encouraged crops to grow,
Harrowed all the grass in spring,
soon as the Daff's appear,
Cattle would be turned out,
and sold that big fat steer.

Job to know where to start,
and find things long forgotten,
Things we used like brushing hooks,
n' pitch forks stale gone rotten,
Shovels spades and muck forks,
all standing where last used,
Some I've had a long time,
and some they were abused.

Workshop that's a nightmare,
the scrap ruck will increase,
Wading through the junk to find,
that lost now found tailpiece

All the things you save as spares,
but things move on apace,
Out dated now and far too small,
with newer one replaced

The tractor that's seen better days,
reliable it has been,
Well used and got a loader on,
could do with a dam good clean,
Worked it hard all day long,
every day of the year,
Last day now it has arrived,
and to the field must steer.

A second one it's older still,
with a draughty cab,
Tyres worn and torn about,
n' the paints a little drab.
Steering wobbles brakes no good,
useful to have about,
Its winter when it wonner start,
I have a dam good shout.

Be sorry to see an empty yard,
and all the cleaned out sheds,
The damp old house abandoned,
and empty old farmstead,
Silence now for few a weeks,
until new folk move in,
Then once again start from new,
new livestock make a din.

If we could sell our experiences for what they cost us, we'd all be millianaires.
Abigail Van Buren (1918)

Chapter 41

Mother reared her Chickens, late in the 1940's

Mother bought her day old chickens from a hatchery, ready sexed so she knew that they would be all pullets, though just the occasional a few would turn out cockerels.

In her order for two hundred they seemed to send half a dozen extra, so it could be they just chucked in a few cock chickens just for the hell of it, after all they had to get rid of them somehow, and being a laying hybrid, they were not much good for fattening. The hatchery would notify us what time they would arrive at our local train station for us to pick them up as promptly as possible. The station master and porters would take the boxes off the train (all steam trains back then) and if it were a cold day stand them by the coke stove in the waiting room, thinking they were doing us a favour, but all it did was to sweat them up then they would get a chill when put in the brooder. The brooder was a mushroom shaped with a curtain round the edge and a cardboard ring outside that to retain the chicken in for the first few days. This was heated with a paraffin lamp down in the centre leg and a thermometer stuck down a hole into the area occupied by the chickens.

Mother had a Brooder

Mother had a brooder,
for her chickens to rear,
Ordered from the hatchery,
had them twice a year,

Two hundred chicks day old,
they dispatched by rail,
Pick them up at the local station,
platform they prevail.

Got to be there to meet the train,
in four boxes norm,
If ya late station master,
stand them by his stove too warm,
Sweats them up then chills them,
tho he means no harm,
As day old need a constant warmth,
the brooder will conform.

They start off on newspaper,
with chicken crumbs to peck,
And a jam jar water fountain,
clean up every speck,
Then to push them under brooder,
paraffin lamp to heat,
Let them out every hour and half,
for them more to eat.

After a day or two they,
go in and out themselves,
Tail feathers start to grow,
into food hoppers delves,
It's a little curtain they go through,
for them warm to keep,
Till they have all their feathers, t
hen onto perches sleep.

Open the hatch to let them out,
first time hour afore dark,
Get then used to where they live,

in and out of the ark,
Soon they grow and forage around,
all about the farm yard,
Laying in the nest boxes, some lay away,
to find them's hard.

In autumn the pens were taken up,
onto field wheat stubble,
Pick up all the grain that shead,
move the pens no trouble,
Field pens with little cast wheels,
slatted floors the lot,
No cleaning out just move the pen,
three times a week new plot.

Month or six weeks then inside,
deep litter pen now ready,
Now the days are shorter,
the eggs flagging off to steady,
New idea, put on a light,
keep them wake much longer,
Time switch bought for this job,
keep up the profits stronger.

This was the first time we had ever had a time switch, and the very up to date thinking was to extend the day for the laying hens, to increase egg production. Never been heard of before, and others in the village could not understand why our hen pen lights were on right up to midnight.

Do not count your chickens before they are hatched.
Aesop (620-560 BC)

Chapter 42

Potatoes planted a foot apart - was not twelve inches

On the up side it meant that three men could plant more potatoes than six people with different size feet. Potatoes', Going on from what Matthew Naylor wrote about potatoes, in one of his blogs, the earliest I remember at home was of the ground being ridged in shallow ridges and for the muck to be spread along and potatoes dropped in the bottom and the ridges split.

He was talking about how his dad always planted them a foot apart, and that was what I recalled, the trouble was not everyone's foot was the same length, some of the women working had size five or six boots right up to some men with size twelve boots, and that's a big difference. You see taters were carried in an apron sack tied round your waist and the bottom two corners had a loop of cord tied to them and was strung up round your neck, this way you could carry half a hundred weight. Each step you took you dropped a spud against your toe, and then step forwards with your heel against the one just dropped and so on. So as you see the plant population varied quite widely from row to row depending on what big footed bloke had planted and another with smaller feet, so overall there could easily be a rough average of a foot apart (in the meaning twelve inches)

When we got onto a tractor ridge plough, we had a potato planter mounted onto it; this consisted of two hoppers for the seed and two seats hanging out the back. Behind one outside furrow was a measuring wheel with a bell on it, to indicate when to drop a spud. It could be varied as to what spacing you required, but it all came down to planting at a foot apart. The seed was carefully tipped into the hoppers on the headlands, knocking off some sprouted tubers, then as they were hand dropped at every ping of the bell down a narrow spout some more sprouts were knocked off, the larger tater took longer to rumble down the spout and the smaller ones shot down quickly. So again the distance apart varied, then a tuft of muck or grass blocked the chute and there would be a dozen taters missed. Stop the machine, empty the spout, and go back and plant them in the ridge where it was thought they should have been.

Another drawback was the incessant ringing of the bell particularly if your seat was right over it, and the planter, while it save walking and carrying the seed down the ridges it did nothing to improve accuracy the spacing's. On the up side it meant that three men could plant more potatoes than six people with different size feet. So planting a foot apart started to become nearer to the twelve inches that was aimed for.

The man who nothing to boast of but his illustrious ancestry is like a potato - the best part is underground.
Thomas Overbury (1581 - 1613)

Chapter 43

The two hundred day winter

I was brought up to cater for a two hundred day winters, and rarely did the cows go out until the third week of April. Hay with kale was fed up to the turn of the year then on to hay and stored mangols for the rest of the winter, corn was fed according to the yields

This was the hub of the dairy farming just after the war, a new flat roofed churn dairy was built along with its churn stand seen in the foreground behind it is the engine shed where at one time the open crank oil engine powered all the barn machinery. It also housed the coal /coke boiler for sterilizing the dairy utensils. The higher loft section is where the barn drive shaft went to drive the cake crusher, mangol pulper, chaff cutter, and roller mill to crush the oats.

The sheds to the left were the cow sheds and a similar run of stalls ran to the right as well, but here these buildings stand empty and redundant having had a few hundred years of use. There seems to be four or five additions to these buildings over the years the first being built with very narrow bricks.

Silage took over from hay in the 1960's it being cut direct with a flail harvester loaded green without wilting, this was long stemmed and only bruised and difficult to consolidate, often getting over heated in the clamp. During the early years of clamping molasses was added with water can, then all sorts of powders came in with wild claims as to how they would help the fermentation, but often as not in good weather conditions it was better not to add anything. As the years have progressed spring turn out has got earlier by around three weeks, and the autumn housing later into November bringing it nearer to a one hundred and seventy day winter

Time is measured in portions

Time goes by for ever,
to history that we can't reset,
Minutes made up of seconds,
sixty seconds every minute,

And hours are made up of minutes,
sixty minutes to show,
Days made up of hours,
twenty four in a row.

Week made up of seven days
Monday to Sunday peaks,
A month is one of twelve,
in which it has four weeks,
Spring summer autumn winter,
winter has the snow,
A year it follows the seasons,
four seasons in a row.

A decade that is ten years,
for knowledge to acquire,
A score of years is twenty,
at three score five retire,
A century seems a long time,
for humans to cavort,
Time is measured in portions,
sometimes long or short.

A lifetimes usually shorter,
but it varies quite a lot,
Time on earth it tests you,
before you hit your plot.

By the time a man realizes that maybe his father was right, he usually has a son that thinks he is wrong. Charles Wadsworth

Chapter 44

Garry the bull (1996-2008)

We had a bull a few years ago, we called him Garry, I had seen Garry advertised on the notice board at our local vet's surgery as a quiet Simmental bull good stock getter and easy to handle and seven years old. After taking down the phone number off the bottom of the card, I rang his owner and duly went to see him "at home" and bought him. It turned out that part of his pedigree name was Linaka, so of course it was an obvious choice to shorten it to Garry after the retired footballer of that name.

Garry was a huge size and had to reverse himself out of the trailer when he was delivered to me, and within a few days was turned in with our suckler cows. He seemed a lazy and laid back sort of chap who when the cow he was following had been served once, he cleared off grazing. In fact I thought he was not working half the time but in the first three weeks he had successfully stopped all the cows.

This is Garry in his last year with us

Although he had been grazing on soft meadows with the cows for two years he gradually became lame, it was a growth or a corn that had developed between his cloven hooves in all four feet, one corn on his front foot became very sore and we called the vet for advice. The only thing to do was to drop him with a needle, get him down and do the corns on all four feet, and give a good pedicure at the same time. So an appointment was made and we drove him into the coral ready for the vet, the vet being a young inexperienced girl who had been briefed on how to go about the job. A fair estimate was made of his weight, the dose was calculated and loaded into the syringe, Garry was trapped behind a gate, (behind a gate because if he went down in the race he would be trapped) and his dose administered.

It gradually took effect and he should have gone down within ten minutes, after half an hour he was still standing swaying around with his front feet well splayed out making it impossible to push him down, even with some rope tied round his legs he still thwarted our effort to fell him, a further small dose was given but to no effect.

The job was abandoned; Gary was left in the coral to recover for a couple of hours, and a vigorous discussion was held with the vets. A further appointment was made and a senior vet came to resume the job that was started four days before. The same estimations were made as to his weight, and the medication was upped to a sure fire level of knocking him out. Just the same thing went on again with Garry splaying his front feet way out as if in an earth quake, and he still would not go down. So after ten minutes he was jabbed again, almost a kill or fell dose, we were told it was dangerously close to a lethal dose, and another ten minutes with his legs well bound, he finally went down.

Garry's head was pulled round and up to him shoulder, and held there while all his operations took place, we file and trimmed his hoof soles, and the vet got his knife out and cut the worst corn off, sprayed with purple spray and bound it to keep it clean and to stem the flow of blood. The other three feet the corns were frozen, with an aerosol the like that plumbers use to freeze a pipe to stop water flow when repairing a pipe. The worrying bit now was the reverse injection, and how soon he would get up, in fact it was the best part of an hour before he did stagger to his feet, stayed in the coral for another three hours, then he was loosed back onto the meadows, with his bandaged foot, being swung wide as he could not make out what had happened to him.

After five or six days his bandage gradually unfurled and dropped off and he started to walk freely once again. Garry's time came to an end when those same corns grew again, and the replacement heifers of his were needing another bull, so regrettably he was dispatched off to meet his maker.

During the last foot and mouth outbreak in the 1990's we were forced to retain a bull calf out of one of our own cows, an Aberdeen Angus bull, we used him and kept a few replacements from him, as we had done with the charolais bull before him. Then more recently we had a Hereford bull off a neighbour who is a breeder, so you can see from any photo's we have of our cows they are all beef bred, a total mixture of breeds, I like to think we have, hybrid vigor.

There's always one in every herd

There's always one in every herd,
who won't respect the fence,
The one that's bold and watches out,
not much common sense,
Test the boundary, test the posts,
test rotten barbed wire,
That bit of grass just out of reach,
the best she must acquire.

Gather the herd all round a gate,
she's the one looking at you,
Ready to bolt and dodge and run,
a test you think she knew,
She gets away the others follow,
guess who's in the lead,
To the furthest corner of the field,
just another stampede.

The electric fence its no use,
the shock she can withstand,
Pushing the wire two yards beyond,
break the single strand,
The other cows they follow her,
they know she's got the knack,
Of how to beat the system,
and always first to the rack.

Suckler Cows

The suckler cows they graze all
summer, until we wean the calf,
When the calves we take away,
cows they bellow not by half,
The calves the same in shed we keep,
until they settle in,
Gates are high and fences too,
all to stop them from escapin.

Three days it lasts, until they feel,
the pain of hunger's stronger,
The cows they clear off down the field,
and hang about no longer,
Calves have no choice but stay,
feed them corn and feed them hay,
One month they need get used to living,
in the yard all in a bay.

They all get wormed and gain no weight,
till frettin they've forgotten,
Put them out on clean grass,
feed supplements, no silage rotten,
There they will grow and gain the weight,
they lost plus plenty more,
When at last they do get fat,
read the scales its there we can't ignore.

Don't take the bull by the horns, take him by the tail, then you can let go when you want to.
Josh Billings (1818-1885)

Church Farm where I first started farming 1960's.

On the right of the picture is the cowshed that tied up 26 cows.

This book continues in Volume 4 of
"The Longest Swath"

It includes , the Village Mortuary, A farmer's Skills know no Bounds, How we Lived in the Old House, We Wuz Brung up proper, grandma's very best Strong float and the cow that Carries its own fence, and many more tales and stories about the village and its people, as well as the cattle and fields around the parish.

5754152R00115

Printed in Great Britain
by Amazon.co.uk, Ltd.,
Marston Gate.